BABY

A

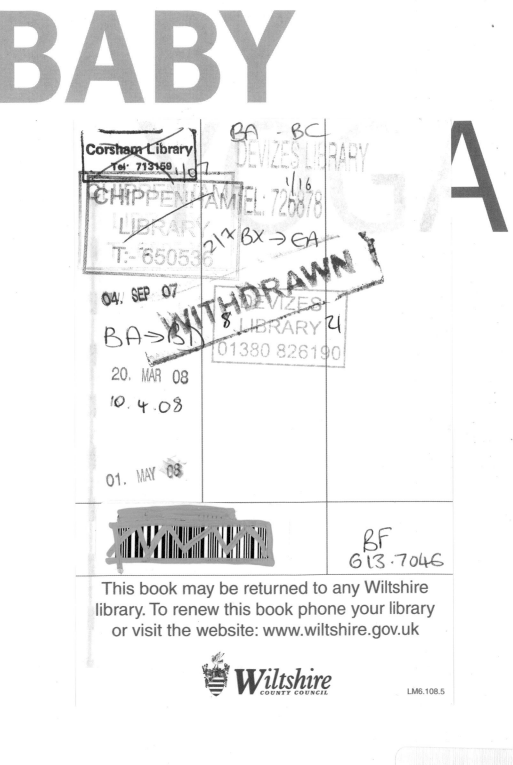

BABY
YOGA

Françoise Barbira Freedman

Foreword by Vimala McClure
Founder, The International Association of
Infant Massage Instructors

To Luke, whose enjoyment of baby yoga was an inspiration to teach it, and to all the babies in Birthlight classes since.

A GAIA ORIGINAL

Books from Gaia celebrate the vision of Gaia, the self-sustaining living Earth, and seek to help its readers live in greater personal and planetary harmony.

Editor	Sarah Chapman
Designer	Sarah Theodosiou
Illustrator	Lucy Su
Photographer	Christine Hanscomb
Managing Editor	Pip Morgan
Production	Lyn Kirby
Direction	Patrick Nugent

Publisher's acknowledgements
Gaia Books would like to thank the following:
Susanna Abbott for editorial assistance and Mary Warren for proofreading and indexing.

Dr. Shamima Owen, Paediatrician at Great Ormond Street Hospital, London, and Dr. Robert Surtees, Consultant Paediatrician and Reader in Paediatric Neurology at The Institute of Child Health, London, for their information and expert advice.

And all the wonderful mothers and babies who posed for the photographs.

GAIA

First published in the United Kingdom in 2000 by
Gaia Books Ltd, 66 Charlotte Street, London W1P 1LR

A catalogue record of this book is available from the British Library.

Printed and bound in China

10 9 8 7 6 5 4 3

Publisher's note
The publisher and author specifically disclaim any responsibility for any liability, loss or risk which may be claimed or incurred as a consequence, directly or indirectly, of the use of any of the contents of this publication.

Cautionary note to the reader
If your baby has any health problems or special conditions, seek medical advice before practising the exercises in this book. Always observe the cautions given, go through each step gently, and never rush any movement. It is best to consolidate the basic sequences through regular practice. As you practice the baby yoga throughout this book, never use force but respond to your baby's enjoyment at his or her own pace.

The worldwide availability of this book in the English language has made it necessary to adopt US spellings in certain circumstances, for example, cesarean, fetal, color.

Contents

Foreword

In 1976–1978, when my babies were born, it was important for me to be able to continue my yoga practice. There were two ways I did this. One was to develop an infant massage routine in 1976 from what I had learned working in India in 1973 and as a yoga instructor from 1970 to 1976; this eventually became my book, *Infant Massage: a Handbook for Loving Parents* (first published in 1978, then in 1982, 1988, and an all new third edition in 2000) and now a worldwide organization of instructors, the International Association of Infant Massage. The other was to incorporate my babies into my yoga routine. I did this in many of the ways Françoise shows in this book. 'Asking Permission' and 'Touch Relaxation' are two of the techniques I developed within the routine my organization now teaches worldwide, and I am glad that Françoise has incorporated a touch of these elements in Baby Yoga. She also includes several of the traditional techniques used with infants in their daily care in India.

I have always been impressed and influenced by the baby rearing practices of indigenous cultures around the world, after all, most of them have had thousands of years more experience than we in the Western world have had, so their wisdom is not to be brushed off as 'tribalism'. I am delighted that Françoise has the expertise and experience to share with you how to do a yoga practice and involve your baby in it. We are often so afraid of the delicacy of our infants that we deprive them of the simple joy of movement and touch, confining them to a reality of angles and planes rather than the beating, breathing, 360-degree world in which they live. We leave them alone, giving them the message that being alone and untouched is a natural state when it is not; many of the inventions of recent times for parents have served to distance us, rather than bring us closer, to our babies as living, breathing, loving beings with whom we have a primary relationship.

As parents, it is very important that we listen to our inner guidance or intuition about what is right for us and for our children. I encourage you to read this book, take a class if one is offered near you, and if you have any questions about the instruction here be sure to check with your healthcare provider before proceeding. Some babies will love the types of movements here, some will need modifications that are more gentle, slow, and encompassing. Particularly, if you have any safety concerns, it is important that you first follow your inner wisdom and consult with people you trust about the safety of any of these practices for your particular baby.

Baby yoga can be a fun and loving way to interact with your child, giving the baby a three-dimensional feel for the world, a sense of the nature of the world as contraction-and-expansion, and a feeling of being in synchronicity with you, the most important person in his or her life. Ideally, you will begin any stretching movements you do with your baby with a warming massage, just as before you begin a workout you warm up your own muscles. Follow your baby's cues and respond to them, using the techniques in this book to guide you in creating your own routine with your baby. I'm sure you will find it as fun, as nourishing, bonding, and relaxing as I did, and that your relationship with your child will benefit immensely by it.

Vimala McClure
Author, *Infant Massage: a Handbook for Loving Parents*, *The Tao of Motherhood*, *The Path of Parenting*
Founder, The International Association of Infant Massage Instructors

Preface

Yoga with babies is part of my life. It has brought together my practice of yoga and what I learned about parenting from Amazonian forest people, both before and after I became a mother. I first thought of baby yoga as physical play, an expansion of the daily massage and bathtime at home for sedentary living in a northern clime. Sequences developed with each baby, and Luke, my fourth child, was such a happy yoga baby that friends soon joined in what was to become a little practice group. To this day, baby yoga classes keep this friendly atmosphere because doing yoga together induces shared pleasure, relaxation and closeness among those doing it.

The two books that influenced me the most as a new mother were Jean Liedloff's *The Continuum Concept* (1975) and Frédéric Leboyer's *Loving Hands* (1977). Both introduce western parents to other traditions in which communication with babies is achieved through physical contact and active handling. Their message corresponded to my experience as a young anthropologist helping to care for my Amazonian sisters' babies. When I gave birth in England, what I experienced in the hospital was deeply alien, and yoga with babies became a way of creating harmony between these approaches to parenting in my experience. As I gained further understanding of yoga through practising and teaching it, I became motivated to develop baby yoga in a way that was faithful to the core aspects of classic yoga. I believe that yoga with babies not only promotes health but also lays a foundation for non-violence and well-being.

Françoise

Introduction

This book presents exercises for babies from birth onwards, adapted from classic Hatha yoga postures. In yoga the body is stimulated and stretched in order to be able to relax better, and the resulting well being induces a deeply felt harmony between the self and the universe. All these benefits are true for babies too.

Yoga applied to babies offers physical stimulation, and will help strengthen the spine, develop supple joints and enliven all the body's systems. Yoga postures also involve the senses, mind and psyche. Similar exercises are traditional in India as a complement to infant body massage, and an integral part of Ayurvedic health care for babies. Baby yoga will give your baby an immediate sense of well-being, and is a mutual process with a great deal of non-verbal communication taking place between you. Even if you have never done yoga before, doing the first sequence with your baby (on pages 32–3) will give you a sense of what yoga does and is about.

The exercises in this book are divided into four phases: from birth to eight weeks, from eight weeks to four months, from four to eight months and after eight months. If your baby is more than eight weeks old when you start, however, it is still a good idea to begin with the routines for new babies before practicing the sequences corresponding to his age. Even if your baby is over eight months old it's not too late to start yoga, but the approach is slightly different and involves more interactive play. Read this book in order to understand how yoga is effective with young babies, before adapting it to your older baby.

Most parents have one baby at a time, and therefore the convention of using the singular is followed in this book. For twins and triplets, however, yoga is an excellent way for them to receive more individual attention and to enjoy each other. Alternating between 'he' and 'she' in successive chapters has been chosen as a way to keep the sexes in balance.

Doing yoga with babies can be effectively combined with postnatal postures, to help women re-align and strengthen their bodies after childbirth. If you have never done yoga before, trying the postures for your baby shown in this book may inspire you to find a yoga class just for you. However limited or extensive your experience of yoga, you will find that your baby has a lot to teach you.

1 How yoga can help your baby

The experience of movement combined with touch is possibly the richest stimulation we can offer babies from birth. In yoga, this stimulation occurs through the mutual involvement of parent and baby, at a pace at which the baby can absorb and integrate it. As yoga postures induce deep relaxation in adults, so in babies they bring about a state of great contentment, and promote peaceful deep sleep.

In the increasingly fast pace of the modern world, our babies need all the help we can give them in order to create a foundation of well–being that will serve them all their life. Yoga offers babies a resource that will enable them to deal positively with stress and know how to relax. Our handling of babies in yoga is a loving one, in which the conversion of a challenging movement into a safe game, to play and enjoy, is repeated again and again. This playful stimulation through yoga-based exercise is the best possible way of helping babies relish life, with all its demands, as they grow.

The combination of touching, stroking, handling and movement brings about a powerful multisensory stimulation for babies. Touching alone has been shown to improve the function of all the body's systems (respiratory, circulatory, digestive, eliminative, nervous and endocrine). Evidence from experiments with a wide range of mammals has shown the importance of physical stimulation for overall healthy development. In comparison with the deprived animals in the control groups, the stimulated animals thrived physically; they gained weight faster, were more alert, looked better and showed a higher immunity to disease. They were also more relaxed, less irritable and less easily frightened than those in the control groups.

Tactile stimulation also contributes to the development of the brain and nervous system, which is not yet complete at birth. In a hospital study in Florida, premature babies who were massaged and rocked daily showed more mature neurological development than those who were not stimulated. Practicing yoga enhances the developmental process, strengthening all functions of the nervous system.

Well–being and health

In yoga every stretch is countered by relaxation, and so your baby will learn that tension and relaxation are complementary. This means that she will be able to experience deep relaxation actively, as a state different from either waking or sleeping. The more babies experience this state, the better they can regulate their response to the tension that inevitably accompanies physical discomfort, particularly of the gastrointestinal system. The colic suffered by many young babies is often caused by the tension of learnt discomfort that builds up and is never fully released from the body. Watching a completely relaxed baby after yoga is an inspiring experience for any parent, reminding us of what is possible.

Babies enjoy and benefit from the cumulative effects of touch, movement, rhythm and relaxation, and as parents we share in this enjoyment and these benefits. Doing yoga with a baby means playing, stretching, and then relaxing together, each participant focusing on the other. You will also receive the benefits of tactile stimulation and relaxation, both through feedback from your baby and from the action itself. Regular yoga practice with your baby will at the same time tone your own muscles, and help balance the successive hormonal changes that follow childbirth, which affect all mothers to some degree.

Yoga and massage

Yoga with babies goes hand in hand with massage. Ideally, massage comes first as a spontaneous extension of the desire many mothers feel to check their baby's body over with their hands just after birth, discovering her with touch, making sure she is all there. Many cultures use massage as a part of baby care. In India, for example, the traditional custom is to give the baby a daily massage with oil, followed by yoga and finally a hot bath, starting from birth. Both massage and yoga are practiced very energetically in India, but have been adapted here to be more gentle for western parents.

You may wish to start each yoga session by giving your baby a full body massage first. A simple massage sequence is shown on pages 30–1. If you don't feel attracted to massage or feel it might take too long to do both, start directly with yoga. It may lead you to massaging your baby later on. Nearly all the sequences include some dry massage, which you do without having to undress your baby or use oils. Every time your baby does yoga, her hands, feet and abdomen are massaged, so she will receive a good deal of massage even if you don't give her a full body massage.

Healing through yoga

Yoga stimulates not only the whole physical body, including the nervous and endocrine systems, but also the subtle energy fields beyond the body itself. If as a mother you did yoga in pregnancy, you already know the power of deep breathing both to stimulate and calm your unborn child, who has carried this knowledge through birth into the outside world.

Yoga engages all the memories and consciousness inscribed in your baby's nervous system since her earliest development. Deep relaxation, especially with her mother, allows the baby to draw upon this continuity. While young babies in other cultures who still spend most of the day and night in close physical contact with their mothers have this continuity passively, it is deliberately recreated in the relaxation that is part of yoga.

Yoga with babies can thus benefit all parents and all babies, even if the birth was difficult. By moving and relaxing together during yoga, you will help heal the memory of a traumatic birth experience as much as you will enhance that of an ecstatic one. In the same way, you can use relaxation with your baby to renew bonding, which may have been disrupted during or after the birth.

Fathers too
Much of the literature on bonding has been concerned with the mother and infant bond, but bonding with the baby is important for fathers too. Both massage and yoga are ideal ways for fathers to have a creative physical rapport with their babies, actively following and contributing to their development.

Sensing the world

While everyone agrees that babies need sensory stimulation for healthy growth, there is a controversy about the source of stimulation and the amount, form and quality of stimulation that are of most value. In some cultures, such as Japan, babies traditionally receive little external stimulation during the first six weeks after birth. By contrast, in America and Europe, babies are surrounded by toys designed to stimulate their senses from birth with an abundance of primary colours and sharp noises.

The first sensory stimulation that yoga offers babies is a slightly more intense and lively version of the ordinary rapport they have with their parents. Babies love human faces, and use all their senses to distinguish their mothers' faces and, if their fathers are often around, their faces too. As you do yoga with your baby, you'll find that she will look back at you when you look at her; if you also talk or sing to her she will respond; she will also smell you more intensely during movement. Your baby is sensitive to touch and the way she is handled, and will quickly learn to distinguish your unique way of holding her.

After touch, sight is intensely stimulated in yoga as the parent's face draws near and then moves further back in movement. The baby learns to change her focus within a short time through the various postures. It would be misleading to try and isolate or prioritize one or another sense. A baby's experience of yoga can best be described as a synesthetic one, in which all the senses are stimulated together and heighten one another.

Yoga also offers 'vestibular stimulation', which is related to balance and experience of altitude. The adaptation of yoga principles to carrying infants and moving with them brings to closer attention forms of stimulation that have been babies' birthright throughout human evolution, but which may be neglected to some extent in the modern world.

The way in which babies respond to their parents' voices, eyes, touch and smell is also directly related to the emotion they associate with the experience. The more parents deliberately engage their own senses while doing yoga with their babies, the greater the babies' response will be. What is important is that all sensory stimulation in yoga takes place in the safety of the parent's arms, with a warm and loving attitude. The aim with yoga is to enhance babies' pleasurable sensations as much as possible. Sensory stimulation is a by-product of the rich and intense interaction that yoga with babies creates, rather than a goal in itself.

The benefits of baby yoga

Physical
• In one short session, your baby is given as much physical activity as she would receive if you handled and carried her all day. All this activity will help her sleep more deeply.
• Your baby's behaviour will be more 'settled'.
• It provides a daily routine of activity through which you can engage constructively with your baby from birth.

Physiological/developmental
• All your baby's bodily systems are stimulated, including the digestive and nervous systems.

Psychological
• Baby yoga helps you and your baby get to know each other, enhancing communication between you.
• Yoga helps to heal any birth trauma; your baby will also be better equipped to deal with shocks.
• Your baby's enjoyment of the positive stress of yoga will increase her ability to cope with future challenges.
• Through the high quality of the attention she receives from her parents, your baby learns to interact with others and play actively.
• The deep relaxation that is part of yoga helps parents cope with the stresses of early parenting.

Enhancing communication

Doing yoga is 'talking' to your baby, non-verbally as well as verbally. Most of us have to learn from our newborns how to communicate with them. In order to do this, we have to be receptive to what our baby is experiencing. We have to forget some of our conditioning about baby care, and try to immerse ourselves in our baby's sensory world and her responses to it. In yoga, it is communication with your baby that stimulates her most. Always be aware that you are not doing yoga *to* your baby but *with* your baby.

Self-awareness and receptivity

The first step in preparing to do yoga with your baby is simply to watch her and listen to her, becoming aware of your own senses and your being in response to her. Two simple practices that link the physical and meditative aspects of classic yoga can help you lay a sound foundation for exercising with your baby.

The Mountain pose

Classically, Tadasana, the Mountain pose, is the beginning and end of all the standing poses that you would do in an adult yoga session. At a time when the arrival of your new baby can change your whole life, Tadasana helps you to be 'there' for yourself and therefore also for your baby. At regular intervals, wherever you are, stop, stand, take a breath, exhale and feel yourself 'be'.

- Stand with your feet together or slightly apart and firmly planted. Feel your spine as upright as possible. If it helps you, bend your knees and align your spine against a wall first.

- Relax your shoulders, neck and arms and look straight ahead. Be aware of your alignment along a vertical axis.

- As you stand between earth and sky, breathing freely, let yourself be intensely in the fullness of the present moment. Refresh yourself, finding the earth under your feet and a new horizon in front of you.

With practice, you can experience the feeling of Tadasana even without standing, whenever you find yourself absorbed in preoccupations instead of being just here in the 'now'.

Breathing awareness

When babies express discomfort by crying, they sense how we respond to them through our body language. A baby's crying is meant to spur us into action and do something to get the crying to stop. In response to crying, stress hormones are released into our bloodstream, increasing our blood pressure, breathing rate and muscular tension. Gaining awareness of our breathing is a powerful tool for avoiding a build-up of tension when it occurs.

Next time your baby cries, even though he has been fed and nothing you do seems to help, try this practice, in any position.

- Firstly, become aware of your breathing. It is likely to be fast and shallow if you are getting tense. Exhale deeply two, three or more times, voicing your out-breaths if needed as 'haah', 'haah'.

- Now take a deeper breath, involving your abdominal muscles. If you don't know how to breathe abdominally, put a hand on your stomach and feel your inhalation pushing your abdomen against it, your exhalation deflating it. Enjoy the very action of breathing in and out fully. Feel your whole body getting involved in the flow of your breath, or Vinyasa.

After just a few breaths, return to your baby's needs; you are now much more likely to decipher and meet them than before. If you feel calm, you will be able to convey this feeling to your baby, and offer her a sense of security and peace.

Letting go of worry

A great deal of worry about our babies' welfare is due to our lack of familiarity with them. Many mothers, let alone fathers, have never held a baby until they have their own, and they often feel confused by so much conflicting advice from experts and others. It is easy to forget that the source of a baby's greatest contentment is simple, physical, sensory communication from you, her parent.

To enable you to 'talk to your baby with yoga', it is helpful to eliminate unnecessary worry. While you may have valid concerns, concern and worry need not go hand in hand. Your concern will guide you to action, and you can 'undo' your worry to a large extent by breathing awareness with the following visualization.

- With each exhalation, let go of the worry, the total heap of the little or big worries of your day and your life at the moment.

- With each inhalation, catch sight of the blue sky over this 'worry cloud'. Inhale and let go again so that you can be more in your body now, just as your baby is and wants you, needs you to be.

'Baby yoga is so mutually beneficial for Katy and me – she loves the attention and rewards me with lots of smiles. Baby yoga teaches us to listen to our babies and discern what they are trying to communicate to us.'

Acknowledging emotions

Nothing can prepare you for the emotions you experience at your baby's birth. What follows a birth, especially that of a first baby, is uncharted emotional territory for all new parents in our culture, and yet, once the baby has been passed fit to go home, with cards, flowers and presents, we are expected to find our own way.

Keeping in touch with your baby every day through close contact, playful interaction and joint relaxation reminds you that you are changing together and that this can be very exciting. Remaining connected with your baby is the recipe for living, rather than merely 'coping', in the first four months.

New mothers are particularly vulnerable because of hormone changes, lack of sleep and the overall responsibility for feeding. New fathers, however, can be equally challenged, and will also find that yoga offers a means of nurturing and expanding their connection with their baby. Often, as a result, it also allows couples to communicate better as they develop their parenting skills.

Quieting the mind

One of the main goals of yoga is to stabilize fluctuating emotions, to open the heart while quieting the mind. The practice of yoga is known to enhance the production of endorphins and prolactin, hormones that induce a feeling of calm contentment and well–being. Yoga with babies encourages daily close physical interaction between parent and child, which ideally complements the quieter intimacy of massage and bath time. Joint relaxation after yoga with your baby can be another powerful tool, besides breathing awareness, through which you can discover or recover the inner source of 'infant joy'.

'I feel that baby yoga has dispersed all the stresses and tensions we both carried from the pregnancy, a protracted labor and the initial few weeks after the birth.'

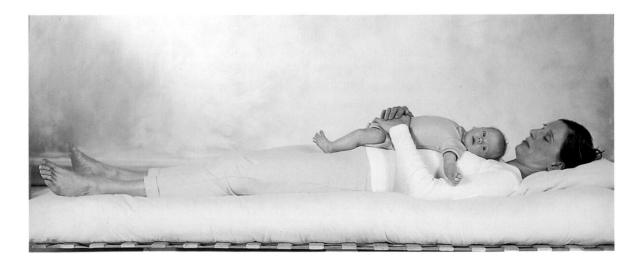

Deep relaxation in yoga also opens a space in which feelings can be acknowledged and then diffused and integrated. If you find yourself trying hard to be the perfect parent, you may seem to be doing well to others but still feel a failure; or you may become depressed, either for a few hours of 'baby blues' or with a deeper sense of inadequacy, when you wonder how to get through the day. You may need regular moments of physical 'letting go' to release stress and to acknowledge your emotions, positive and negative.

Calming meditation

If you find yourself feeling a range of unwanted emotions or if you find it hard to go back to sleep after a night feed, it may help to do the following simple exercise.

- First of all, try and feel any distress as you acknowledge it. Say silently what you feel, and experience it in your body. Then think of the opposite, positive emotion. Sometimes it is not easy. Name it aloud, hearing yourself say it, several times if need be.

- Now focus on your heart, the source of your baby's emotional nourishment. Close your eyes and on each out-breath, let this positive emotion expand in any shape, form or color. Watch it expand and secure it in your heart before you open your eyes again.

This practice will not resolve issues about which you feel strongly; they will still need to be addressed. But it will give you a different perspective, and enable you to avoid trapping and churning negative emotions inside you at a time when you may feel more isolated than usual, with fewer opportunities to share your feelings with friends.

Self-referral

Through practicing yoga relaxation, we learn to perceive how our baby reflects our moods, and to avoid projecting a low mood on to our baby. This is the principle of 'self-referral', looking into oneself first when our emotions are stirred during an interaction. Because we are already developing unconditional love for our baby, she can be our best teacher of 'self-referral'. Acknowledging our emotions frees us from hiding the truth from ourselves, and it frees our baby from the confusion between our feelings and our overt messages to her. Babies always respond to true feelings and sometimes it is good to talk to them, because they will receive the loving intent in your honesty. Compassion and empathy are also qualities that our babies can best teach us.

Your baby's emotions
Babies express emotion with their bodies. The waving hands of a newborn or the kicks of a four-month old are obvious signals, but you can discover many others as you become more attentive to your baby's moods. The rewards are immediate and great, as we can decipher better and better the many different ways our baby cries, and meet his needs more directly and fully.

The 'expanding spiral of joy'

The more happiness you give your baby, the more happiness you will receive from her. This is the expanding spiral of joy. Early parenthood may often be ridden with anxiety, if external pressures and lack of self-confidence undermine our faith in our abilities and our joy in our babies. Doing yoga with your baby will defuse this anxiety and help create an expanding spiral of joy, a positive process that creates shared happiness and harmony between you. Follow the steps below, starting in the middle of the spiral at number 1.

1 Touch and movement foster communication between parent and baby

• Sensory stimulation is inseparable from 'affect' – babies receive sensory input with feelings, such as comfort/discomfort, pleasure/pain, security/fear.

• Babies are highly sensitive to our emotions and respond to them intensely.

5 As the spiral expands, we gain

• Enhanced communication.

• Well–being, and the shared experience of well–being.

• Trust.

• A sense of fun, so that we see playing with babies as the most important activity.

• A positive attitude to life: life is to be enjoyed to the full.

4 In the 'expanding spiral of joy' parents can forget about other people's expectations, and simply enjoy their baby's enjoyment of life. This is the best source of joy in parenting.

6 Through the expanding
spiral, parents rediscover

• The power of creative play.

• The magic of finding delight in
  another person's delight.

• The physical counterparts of
  positive emotions.

• That parenting is the creation
  of mutual growth day by day.

• The underlying current of love
  that sustains us through the
  ups and downs and changes
  babies take us through.

• That we must surrender to
  being there for our babies
  and ourselves, just as we are,
  with the emotions of the
  moment, whatever they
  are now.

2 With touch and movement,
babies experience pleasure
in a physical way, enjoying
their bodies.

• We experience their
  pleasure and reflect our
  delight to them.

• They receive our delight
  and are fulfilled.

3 This process is expanded in
a wider and wider spiral as
we increase our repertoire of
yoga exercises, and relaxation
allows us to integrate positive
experiences with our babies,
healing residual stress and
even minor traumas.

7 Each day's surrender expands
the spiral a little more for
tomorrow.

2 From cradling to stretching

The first eight weeks after a baby's birth are an intense time, and the practice of baby yoga can help meet your needs as well as your baby's. Yoga is fundamentally about relaxation, and simply feeling your new baby close to you and letting go of all else can be a wonderful way of getting started. You can begin yoga with your baby as soon as you hold him in your arms for the first time.

When you do yoga with your newborn baby, you must meet his needs both for being cradled and for stretching. He needs to stretch and expand the movements that you may remember him doing when he still had space in the womb, and discover how it feels to straighten his spine on his front and back. But he also needs to be cradled, with his back and neck totally supported and his legs bent, just as he also was before birth. The trend for new mothers to be active as soon as possible rather than staying in bed after giving birth has resulted in earlier activity for new babies too, but both mothers and babies need to balance activity with rest. The yoga movements in this chapter provide this balance for both of you in the weeks following the birth.

Yoga with your newborn gently encourages his spine to unfold from its curled fetal position, helping him to gain neck control and his muscles to grow stronger. (A newborn's muscles comprise only a quarter of his body weight, as opposed to about half in an adult.) Through stretching his limbs, your baby will also open up his hip, shoulder, knee and elbow joints.

A yoga session with your baby includes all the components of classic yoga: setting your intent, warming up in preparation for stretching, postures and movements that stimulate the main organs and systems of the body and tone muscles, followed by deep relaxation and perhaps meditation. A sequence of movements will take about 10 minutes, although you may wish to stay in a relaxed state for much longer. With time, as well as doing a daily yoga routine with your baby, you will probably find that yoga becomes part of all your everyday activities, influencing the way you lift and carry your baby, stand up and sit down with him, and relate to him generally.

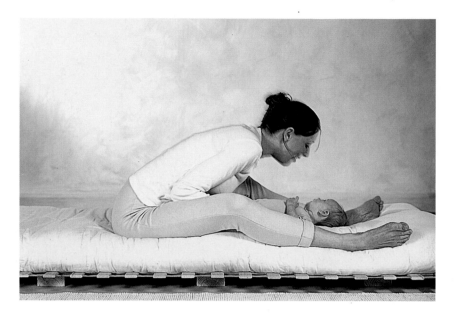

Getting started

The most important factor in getting started is that you do it in a comfortable and mutually rewarding way. Your contact points with your baby are not only your hands and the support of your body but also your eyes, your voice and your awareness. The yoga routine for a new baby is very gentle, becoming more active as your baby gets older. Every baby is different, however, and it is primarily his response, irrespective of his age, that will guide you as to which routine to practice when. Babies do not need to be undressed for yoga, although they enjoy being unconstrained by clothes some of the time, when it is warm enough. Always keep your baby's feet bare, though, not only because it gives you a better hold but also because of the benefits of handling and massaging his feet.

The best time of day

There is no rule about the best time to do yoga with your baby. As you may already have found out or will soon discover, no sooner do you think you have established a routine, than it gives way to another one. Be flexible and do yoga whenever you have the opportunity.

Week by week, yoga will become integrated in your day-to-day handling of your baby, not only through the main exercise routine but also through an 'integrated practice' of yoga-based holding, stretching and relaxing. A few minutes' practice at a time will build up rapidly to establish a foundation that you both develop together. For best results, do a daily practice, however short it is. If either of you are unwell, you can still do relaxation. It can help you keep up yoga until you feel ready to resume the active postures. When you start again, allow a couple of days to get back to where you stopped.

The evening may be the best time to enjoy doing the main routine, especially if your baby is unsettled. Combined with massage and a bath, it will make the baby pleasantly tired and promote deeper sleep. It is also a time when parents can involve siblings and make it a family practice, with everyone enjoying themselves and the baby. Conversely, a morning practice can offer a moment of intimacy and closeness to a parent who has little other spare time, due to work or looking after other children.

The place

Yoga with babies can be done anywhere, both at home and when out visiting with your baby. If you have room, make a yoga corner in your house, where you can have a mat and a couple of cushions or a beanbag, on the floor or on a low bed or futon, ideally next to a space of bare wall for you to stretch against. Your baby's changing mat or table are also suitable for yoga if it is a comfortable height and you have enough freedom of movement. If you prefer to sit on a chair, you can do yoga with your baby lying down on a table in front of you, adjusting your seat to a comfortable height. Putting your baby on a special blanket, mat or sheet, which you can carry with you for use anywhere, can also give your baby a greater sense of continuity and recognition that adds to the familiarity of the yoga routines.

'When I started to do yoga with the twins it was like getting out of a fog. It helped make the bits of the day and night fit together again for me.'

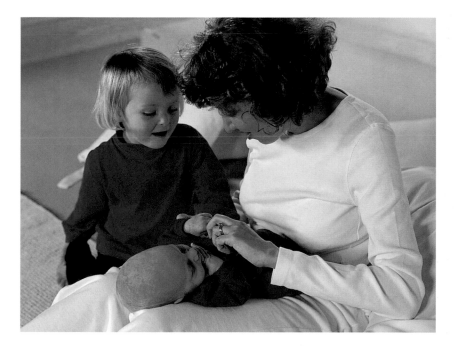

Setting the mood

The right mood and attitude are important when you do yoga with your baby. Sometimes everything seems to be in place, and yet you do not feel like doing yoga. Don't force yourself, or make your baby go through the motions without your full involvement. Since your emotions are part of what will be exchanged between you and your baby, in the early days of your practice it is best to wait until you feel better. Later on, as you become more experienced with relaxation, you will be able to use yoga with your baby to enter 'the expanding spiral of joy', whatever your initial mood or state.

Even if you feel ready, your baby may not be willing. If he is crying or seems unhappy, wait until later. There will be plenty of other times when your baby is ready to enjoy yoga with you. Be attentive to your baby's moods and avoid imposing or forcing anything. The more you do yoga together, the more instantly ready he will be when you are, because he will anticipate the shared pleasure.

Positions for baby yoga

Because your new baby needs as much close contact with you as possible, it's best for you to have your baby on your lap for the first yoga routine. He will feel secure in your physical warmth, and at a distance from you for which all his senses are best equipped. This will also enable you to satisfy both the cradling and stretching needs of your new baby.

First of all, you must be comfortable. Make sure your back is well supported, whether you're in bed, or on a sofa or chair. If you prefer

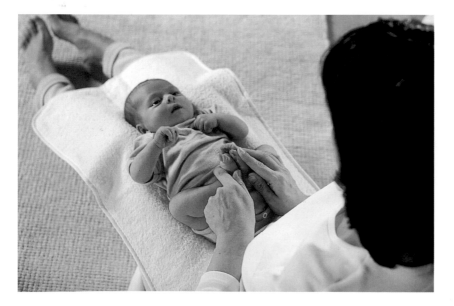

Your baby's character
All babies are different, and change as they grow. As you do yoga with your baby, match your style of practice to your baby's current needs. Sometimes he may enjoy lively, rhythmical movements, sometimes more gentle handling. You will soon develop sensitivity to your baby's unique character. Getting to know your baby means accepting and loving him as he is, and acting accordingly.

to sit unsupported, make sure that you can sit upright without strain. If you have had a cesarean section, take care not to compress your lower abdomen so that you can breathe deeply while sitting. Use cushions of different sizes to help you get into the best position. Your legs can be bent or extended. Your movements during yoga should originate easily from your lower back, so that your energy remains centered in the pelvis as you stretch and bend your arms.

Choose one of the following positions for your first routine. Any of them will help promote your own fitness by enlivening your spine. (This is part of your yoga.)

1 Back upright (whether supported or not) and legs horizontal; your baby lies facing you along your thighs or between your legs.
2 Back supported, reclining about 30-degrees, and knees bent from a right angle at the hips. Your baby lies on your thighs, his head higher than his feet.
3 Lying on your front.

As you get into these positions, become more aware of your spine, dorsal muscles and neck. With your back as straight as possible, feel how breathing deeply and freely involves your abdominal muscles.

Due to a reflex action of his neck, your baby may not sustain eye contact for long, and turn his head to one side. Your baby is not ignoring you; keep 'talking' to him, both verbally and with your hands, even if he looks away. The second position, with your baby lying on your sloping thighs, allows you to keep his head aligned for better eye contact with you.

> **Watchpoints**
> • Is your lower back sufficiently supported?
> • Do you need to raise your baby on a cushion placed on your lap?
> • Can your chest/upper back remain wide open while you place your hands on your baby?
> • Is your neck free of strain?
> • Can you cradle your baby's head and extend your arms over his head comfortably?

Making contact

Whether you are going to combine massage with yoga or just do yoga, you need to 'ask your baby's permission' to involve him by means of a physical message that lets him know your intention to start the session. This involves placing your hands on your baby's body and then gently moving them as described below, either on the abdomen or the feet, or both. According to several traditions of spiritual healing, this helps 'ground' your baby's subtle energies after birth. You may find that your baby prefers one way. Talk to your baby at the same time, perhaps describing what you are doing.

Abdominal circles

This massage stimulates a sensitive area in most babies, partly because of digestion and also possibly because of the adjustment to the cutting of the umbilical cord. Later on, just doing this may calm your baby or toddler when he is upset.

Place one hand flat on your baby's abdomen and take a full breath, inhaling and exhaling. Then use a clockwise motion for circular stroking around your baby's navel with your hand.

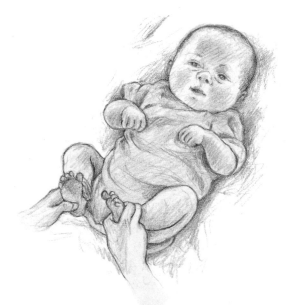

Holding the feet

Every time you hold your baby's feet, you stimulate major reflex points among the 7,000 nerve endings in each foot, and ease the flow of energy through your baby's whole body. If your baby's feet are often cold, stimulating his circulation in this way will warm them.

Hold his feet firmly, one in each hand, and press gently on the soles with your thumbs.

Warming up

If you don't want to give your baby a full body massage (see page 30) before you start your yoga routine with him, do the following 'dry' massage movements instead. They will warm up your baby before yoga, stimulate the circulation and invite him to get into stretching as opposed to cradling 'mode'. You can do them with your baby clothed or unclothed, and they will help you get used to touching and handling your new baby firmly and with confidence.

It is also helpful to have a stretch yourself before you start yoga with your baby to loosen your arms and shoulders. Inhale and extend your arms forward, then exhale. Inhale again and stretch them above your head as you exhale.

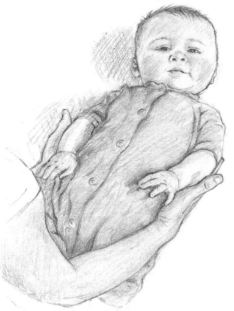

Whole body stroke

This is a sweeping, energetic yet light stroke.

Slide your hands under your baby's shoulders and stroke gently down the spine, moulding his hips and buttocks with both hands as you extend the stroke down the legs.

Repeat several times, watching your baby's reaction. Stop and cuddle him if he cries, and try again later.

Touch relaxation

This reassuring movement is especially important if your baby was premature or had a difficult birth (because he may associate touching with pain).

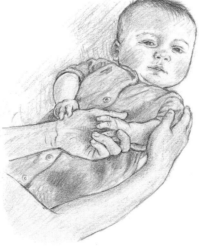

Supporting your baby's arm with one hand, lightly pat his arm with the fingers of the other. In a calm voice, repeat the word 'relax'. When your baby responds, smile and kiss him.

From massage to yoga

The many benefits of giving your baby a full body massage with oil (any pure oil) include an increased sense of security and well–being in your baby, who will feel loved, soothed and cared for. There is a cumulative effect if you follow massage with yoga in the Indian tradition. There is no set way to massage your baby, and you can easily practice the strokes shown here before doing baby yoga. If you prefer not to massage with oil before yoga, do some basic strokes with your clothed baby instead (see page 29). The most important aspect of all massage is that you relax and make it an enjoyable shared experience.

1 Legs and feet

An easy, enjoyable way of starting massage and helping your baby relax all over is with 'Indian milking' of the legs.

Hold one of your baby's ankles with one hand. Make a bracelet with your other hand around your baby's thigh and slide it up the leg to the foot as if milking a cow, alternating your hands in one flowing movement.

Finish by squeezing each toe and stroking the sole of the foot from heel to toe with your thumb.

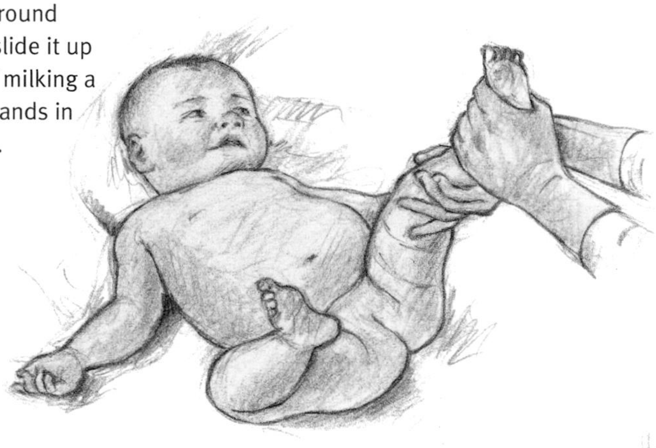

2 Chest

With both hands, stroke the chest from the centre out to the sides, then back to centre in a flowing circular motion. Then, with one hand, stroke diagonally across the chest to each shoulder, then back to centre down the chest.

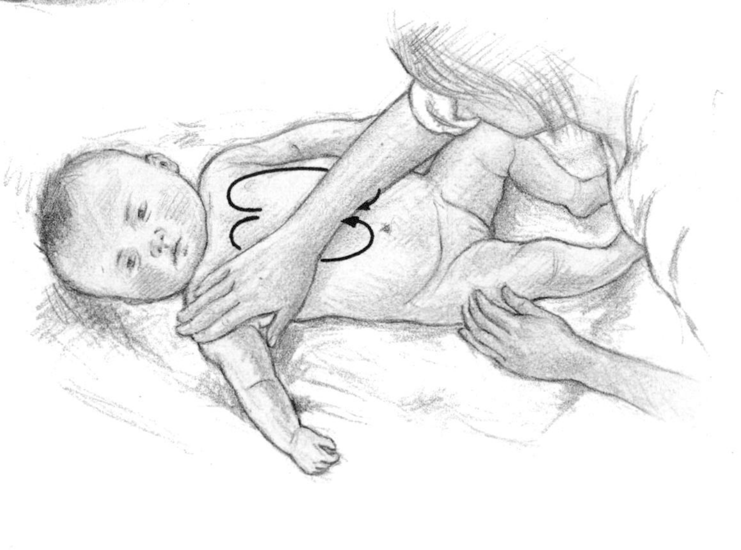

3 Arms and hands

Holding his wrist with one hand, 'wring' the arm from the armpit to the hand, in the same way as for the leg. Squeeze each finger and circle your thumb round the palm.

4 Face

With your hands on the sides of your baby's face, stroke over the eyebrows with your thumbs from the bridge of the nose, and down around the cheeks and jaw.

5 Back

With one hand open, stroke very lightly your baby's back from neck to buttocks, alternating your hands in one flowing movement.

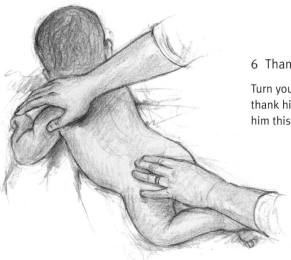

6 Thank you

Turn your baby back over, and thank him for letting you give him this massage today.

The first hip sequence

This first set of movements corresponds to the core of Hatha yoga, which aims to open the hip and knee joints in order to tone the deeper muscles of the body around the base of the spine. This both strengthens and refines the life force in the individual. The conscious use of the breath aids this process for adults, but most babies are an inspiration to us in that they naturally demonstrate unhindered abdominal breathing.

Caution: although babies' muscles have no knots of tension, there is a great deal of variation in the suppleness of their joints. Be gentle and do not force a movement: you may notice that one hip joint is less flexible than the other, which is fairly common.

1 Knees to chest

This posture stimulates the digestive system, and can produce a bowel movement or burp.

Take your baby's legs just under the knees and bend them open, slightly wider than the hips. Press your baby's knees firmly on the sides of his abdomen, just under his rib cage.

Release the pressure and repeat two or three times, taking your time and relaxing completely in between without lifting your hands.

If your baby seems uncomfortable, and his abdomen feels hard, massage it gently and try the movement again later.

2 Knees from side to side

This posture slightly twists the base of the baby's spine.

With your hands in the same position as before, bring the bent knees of your baby together in alignment and move them to the left and then the right.

Press firmly on each side of the abdomen as above, taking your time to release the pressure before changing sides.

3 Pedal stretch

Vary the previous posture by moving the legs alternately toward the rib cage and stretched toward you, in a slow pedalling action.

4 Half lotus

This continues the asymmetrical movement.

Holding your baby's feet, bring the left foot toward the right hip in a half lotus position. Press the heel on the side, wherever it reaches easily.

Release and do the same with the right foot.

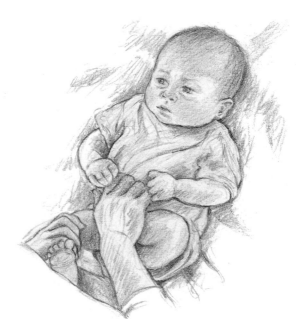

5 Butterfly

This posture opens your baby's hips.

Hold your baby's ankles with both hands and bring the soles of his feet together. Gently push them toward the abdomen.

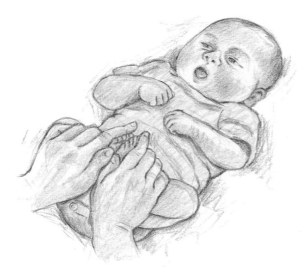

6 Closing the hips

Holding your baby's ankles as before, bring them together, drawing them slightly toward you. Repeat this movement slowly two or three times; your baby's eyes will close as you draw his knees in.

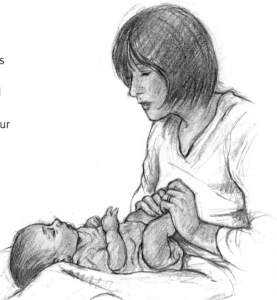

You can now do the dry massage shown on page 29, if you did not do so earlier, before going on to the final movement of the sequence.

7 Leg stretch and drop

This posture shows your baby the contrast between stretching and relaxing by combining both in one movement.

Still holding your baby's ankles, lift his legs very slightly, extending them at the same time, then let them drop loosely.

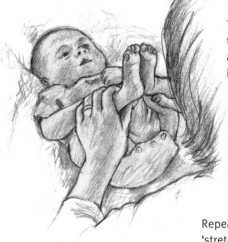

Repeat several times. Say 'stretch' and then 'let go' with your liveliest intonation to make it more fun, and stress the contrast between stretching and relaxing.

This first sequence takes between 5 and 10 minutes. Some new babies are quite tired at the end of it, while others want more. Let your baby guide you as to whether to stop now or continue with another sequence. Whenever you finish, relax deeply with your baby as shown on page 42 (feeding him at the same time if he is hungry) to make an ideal ending to your routine.

Babies' responses to yoga

Doing yoga with your baby stimulates behavior that is part of his normal development, not only increasing its frequency and intensity, but also enhancing it, making it more enjoyable, and eliciting it slightly earlier than if your baby did not do yoga.

Physical responses

Yoga seems to facilitate the transition from reflex to conscious movement in the first six months of life. This may be because of the increased co-ordination of a new baby's back muscles gained from a daily yoga routine. Two indicators of this transition are stretching and kicking. After doing yoga, your baby is likely to start stretching more, with his whole body. The fetal movements of your baby that continue after birth gradually give way to short bursts of more repetitive movements as your baby begins kicking and bicycling actions. These appear to be accelerated by the hip sequence. 'Relaxed holding', particularly face down (see page 36), helps babies strengthen their necks. When you place your baby on his front, he may then practice turning and even lifting his head early on.

Emotional responses

Babies are great communicators. The more you engage your baby, the more he responds and engages you too. A new baby can focus at 30 cm (12 in), the perfect distance for your baby to see your face clearly when you sit with him to do yoga. This often results in an intense exchange between you, as your baby first gazes intently at your eyes and then becomes delighted as you look back at him, particularly if you smile at and talk to him at the same time.

Your voice is another source of delight. As the days go by, you will become less self-conscious about singing or talking to your baby through the yoga routine. Watch how your baby follows your lips intently, and perhaps make his first attempts to talk to you.

Making clicking noises with your baby during your daily yoga routine is also a way to encourage shared communication. Click your tongue several times as clearly and loudly as you can in front of your baby. Wait a moment and do it again. Your baby may start clicking back, perhaps not straight away but later or the next day. Some babies will 'click' for up to half an hour. The received ideas about babies' short concentration span are not confirmed by the experience of shared communication with them after the gentle stimulation that yoga provides.

Babies are very responsive to 'fun' facial expressions and enjoy them a great deal. They are the first trigger to their sense of humor, the frequent source of their first chuckle. Soon after birth, your baby is keenly aware of the difference between your serious face and your smiling face. Be aware of it too, and play with contrasts as part of your yoga routine.

Relaxed holding

Because 'relaxed holding' is a central concept in yoga with babies, it is important to use this position while your baby is still light and easy to carry, and before you have got into the habit of holding him another way. Once you have learned relaxed holding, you will find that, as your baby grows larger and heavier, you can spontaneously adjust the way you hold him without straining your back.

While relaxed holding is helpful to you, your baby benefits even more. When he is 'held relaxed' he can literally relax and enjoy life. This in turn allows you to release any tension you have. In societies where mothers carry their babies everywhere, they 'hold relaxed' without knowing it, usually from an early age. It is humbling to learn it from them. At the same time, it is consistent with the principle of relaxation in action that extends to all yoga.

Basic 'relaxed holding' face-down

Holding babies facing down has only been recommended to western parents in recent years. Many, if not most, babies, however, prefer this position to all others and are immediately pacified by it. One of its main advantages is that it puts comforting pressure on the abdomen, which makes it therapeutic, especially for babies with colic (see page 132).

To hold your baby face-down in a relaxed way, first your shoulders must be relaxed. If you hold your baby too high, your shoulders will be tense. To find the right position for you and your baby, practice this posture while sitting down at first.

This relaxed holding position is a 'safety position' in which you use both hands and various support points to give your baby maximum freedom and stability. It contrasts with other holding positions in which your baby faces you, or has the front of his body against yours. You can adjust this position so that your baby is more or less upright in a 'relaxed seat hold' close to your body, resting on your 'seat hand', or lying across your body with his back against your rib cage so that he faces outwards.

Variations of this safety position will be used in adaptations of standing yoga poses with your baby from this stage onward, throughout his first year.

> **Support points for relaxed holding positions**
> • Your breastbone and top ribs
> • Your arm across the baby's chest
> • The baby's spine supported against you and his head supported in alignment
> • Your hand under the baby's seat

Face-down safety position

With your baby in the basic seat hold (see page 36), hold him firmly against your rib cage. Then slide your baby's chest on to your upper hand and hold his upper arm firmly between thumb and forefinger.

Now place your strong hand, the 'seat hand', between your baby's legs to support his abdomen. Move him face-down, keeping his head aligned with his spine. To give his head additional support, rest it on your forearm.

Rolling variation

Holding your baby in this relaxed face-down position, roll him up and inward to face you (and perhaps give a cuddle or a kiss) and roll him out again face-down. Try this first while sitting before doing it standing up. Start with a very gentle roll and, if your baby enjoys it, increase it gradually to a bigger movement.

Extension of relaxed holding

Once you are confident about supporting your baby in this way, you can hold him more loosely without securing his arm between your thumb and forefinger.

As your baby's neck strengthens, practice supporting only his chest while he hangs over your arm, with your strong hand ready to give additional seat support if needed.

Most babies relax completely in this position (like a kitten being carried by a cat). Observe your baby's response, and experiment with different ways of holding him using these guidelines.

Caution: for extra safety while experimenting, sit on a soft carpet or a bed.

First balances

A number of classic yoga postures involve balancing, not only to promote stretching of the leg and back muscles but also to improve the centering of energy in the body. Balances have positive effects on the nervous system, and are applied to new babies in a very gentle and supported way, before being developed later on. These three balances make a short sequence that you can practice at any time when you have a spare moment. Start in a sitting position and, when you feel confident, try them standing.

Caution: until you feel confident about handling him freely, practice these postures with your baby dressed rather than naked.

1 Cradling seat hold

This pose will help strengthen your baby's spine from sacrum to neck, and co-ordinate the back muscles. Use your strongest hand, the right if you are right-handed and the left if you are left-handed, as a base under your baby's bottom to make a seat.

Stand, kneel or sit (with your baby on your lap sideways) with your strong hand in front of him. Support his head with your other hand, making sure that you also support the base of the neck. This is the upright seat hold for balances with a new baby.

When you feel comfortable, place your open strong hand under the baby's bottom and lift him gently. He is now balancing on your hand, supported by your other hand behind his head. Practice getting your baby as upright as possible and then gradually lessening your support of his head although keeping your hand in position.

Hold the position for a moment before either holding your baby close again or continuing with the following exercises.

2 Mini-drop

Some babies enjoy this straight away, but others may extend their arms in a reflex called the Moro reflex at first, if the drop startles them. The more 'settled' a new baby is, the less he will be startled. The mini-drop, however, is not only an indicator but will also help a baby to become more secure. It can also be an effective way to soothe him.

Do this with your baby in the seat hold as before, or with

your baby facing away from you and your weaker hand as a safe support across your baby's chest, as shown. Lift him up gently with your seat hand and then let your arm drop a little, while continuing to hold him in the same way. Repeat once or twice if your baby enjoys it. Move slowly avoiding any shaking and jostling.

Caution: allow full support of your baby's neck and head with your arm across his chest.

3 Mini-swing

All babies enjoy rocking movements, and benefit from them. This is another extension of the seat hold.

In the same position, swing your baby very gently from side to side in a rocking movement, gradually increasing it to the liking of your baby.

Alternative modes of relaxed holding

The sooner you can hold your new baby comfortably in different ways, the more relaxed you will feel and the more freedom of movement you will have, even when he grows heavier. Ideally, hold your baby on both sides of your body for the sake of symmetry. If you support your baby as described below, however, your posture should not be affected by carrying your baby more on one side than the other.

Relaxed cradling, face-down

Relaxed cradling can induce your baby to fall asleep if you practice it regularly from early on. This is a position in which you can also relax while carrying your new baby.

• From the safety position, bring your baby closer to you and bring the arm of your seat hand between his legs to reach your other hand, holding him in a slightly looser way than the safety position. With his head resting on your bent arm and in the secure comfort of your joining hands, your baby can enjoy falling asleep. Swinging him softly in a rocking movement will be even more soothing.

Upright holding

Holding your baby upright may strain your neck and shoulders if you hold him too high. You will find it more comfortable if you position your baby's whole body firmly against your chest as well as your shoulder. Many babies enjoy falling asleep in this position.

• Start from the seat hold again, with your baby facing you and supporting his head and seat with each hand.

• Now bring him close to your body with his head resting on or just below your shoulder. Use your weaker arm to support your baby's back or shoulder while your strong hand remains under his seat.

• You can also practice mini-drops in this position, lowering and raising him gently towards you.

When holding a new baby upright in a sling, it is a common mistake to carry him too low. This pulls your shoulders forward, causing poor posture and possibly backache. Adjust your position so that the baby's head rests on the centre of your chest, just below your throat. In this way you can fully support your baby on your breastbone.

Relaxed holding in movement

The more ease you feel in carrying your baby as you walk with him, the more he will enjoy it too. It is worth taking time not simply to carry your baby around but to 'walk relaxed' with him, with awareness of your posture, breathing, rhythm and movement.

Lifting

The way you pick up your baby will also become more relaxed with practice. If you get used to rolling him over as for the seat hold, with one arm round his chest and the other ready to support him under his buttocks, you can continue lifting him in this way until he is a toddler. You can easily lift a young baby into the safety position face up, either to be cradled or carried upright.

Aligning your spine

Once you are carrying your baby in a comfortable relaxed position, be aware of the alignment of your spine as you walk. Look at yourself in a mirror if needed, or better, stand against the edge of an open door, bending your knees slightly so that your whole back is straight against the door. New parents tend to lean forward to protect their babies, but your baby will feel more secure if you walk with your chest open and your shoulders back because you will be more stable.

Rhythm and movement

Everyone has one or more rhythms for walking. Sometimes, however, it feels so daunting to hold a new baby that you lose your rhythm. As you walk with your baby, be aware of your center of gravity. Feel your uprightness and symmetry as you walk, putting slightly more weight on the outside of your feet if your arches have weakened during the pregnancy. Rediscover the pleasure of walking, using the entire sole of each foot with every step, and involving all your back muscles in the realignment of your spine.

As you carry your baby 'relaxed', he will follow the movement of your body in walking. This is pleasant for him and is made possible by his supported position against your body. Walking in the right way with your baby also has many benefits for you. It helps you strengthen your spinal muscles and regain – or gain – a sound posture after pregnancy. It refreshes and invigorates you, oxygenates your blood and lifts your spirits. You do not need to go far; going back and forth in your living room or garden is fine to get started. Awareness of your breathing will enliven your walking even more.

Relaxation with a new baby

Relaxation is as much a part of yoga as activity. In yoga with a new baby, the relaxation comes from you at first. You also learn how your baby relaxes by observing him in the process of falling asleep. Gradually, as you gain experience, relaxation becomes a shared skill that you and your baby can practice whenever you need it. The classic yogic relaxation in Shavasana, the Corpse pose, helps to induce deeper rest.

Cradling relaxation

This is an easy way to start if you are new to yoga. Choose a moment when your baby is contented, such as after a feed.

- Sitting down comfortably, lift your baby gently to hold him in the cradling position. Check that your shoulders and neck are relaxed. Sway your baby slightly from side to side and then, holding him firmly against you, twist your spine gently to the right and left. If necessary, support your baby on one or two cushions placed on your lap.

- Look at your baby and at the same time be aware of your heart area, close to your baby's body as he lies against yours. Release any remaining tension in your shoulders and arms with your next exhalation. Feel the close contact between your two hearts.

- You can also relax in this way while standing, or walking slowly counterclockwise in a small circle (see also pages 66–7 for more on walking relaxation).

Feeding relaxation

Breastfeeding contributes to the release of hormones that help you relax. Make full use of these natural processes if you can in the two months following birth. Relaxing before and during feeding facilitates the establishment of breastfeeding. Feeds may also be your best opportunity to relax your baby too, and you may also be able to involve any older children in the relaxation. This exercise makes use of your breathing to release both physical and mental tension.

- Get into a comfortable feeding position, and take a few deep breaths. Allow each exhalation to reach as low down in your abdomen as possible, emptying your mind of its current preoccupations with the out-breath.

- As you inhale, feel your breasts filling and softening with the influx of prana, the universal life force enlivened with yoga. Continue breathing in a slow, steady rhythm while your baby starts feeding.

By breathing deeply into the base of your lungs, gradually your intercostal muscles will expand in your mid-back and enable you to hold your baby more easily without rounding your shoulders. You will also feel better altogether for this deeper breathing, now that the pressure of your diaphragm against your ribs in late pregnancy has disappeared, and your ribs can move freely up and down again as you breathe.

The Corpse pose with your baby

Even if you are familiar with yoga, follow these steps, since relaxing with your baby is different from relaxing alone. You need to lie down comfortably on a firm bed or on the floor. You may need to keep your knees bent and place a cushion under your head so that your whole back rests on the support. Have a blanket to hand in case you need extra warmth.

- Either lie down holding your baby, or lie down first with your baby beside you and then gently place him on your stomach. Have your baby on his back or front, according to his preference. Exhale deeply a couple of times to release tension, and close your eyes.

- If at first you feel insecure if you are not holding your baby, hold him gently with your arms around his body to reassure you, so that you can close your eyes. Be aware of the contrast between how your baby felt inside you and how he feels now, out there, yet close to you.

- Then relax for yourself: acknowledge your own core self and allow yourself to rest for as long as you can.

- Take at least as much time to get back into activity as you needed to relax, if not more. If your baby starts crying, take a couple of deep breaths to get out of relaxation and comfort him.

'Baby yoga has played an essential part in forming Frankie's calm, confident character. Combined with baby massage, I believed it strengthened our physical bond, which I felt was missing initially due to a cesarean birth.'

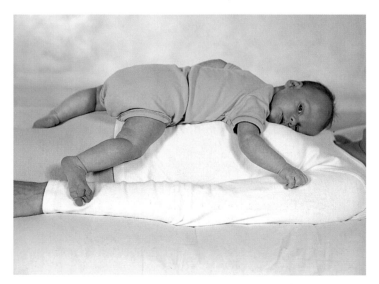

3 Strength and co-ordination

Eight weeks to four months

In two months, you have witnessed the transformation of your helpless newborn into a person increasingly responsive to you and the world, and acquiring more control over her body each day. Your baby may always be ready for action or have a more contemplative temperament. During the next two months, while respecting her unique personality, you can give your baby a balance of activity and quiet with a greater variety of yoga poses.

All babies follow the same sequence of physical development, and yet each baby will do so at her own pace and acquire skills in her own time. This is no reflection of intelligence. It is best to avoid comparisons with other babies or measurements of your baby's performance against charts and norms. Taking pride in your baby for her own sake rather than her achievements is an aspect of unconditional love. When she is clearly thrilled with the latest skill she has mastered, however, your praise will add to her joy.

The study of parenting in other cultures shows us that, from an early age and long before they are able to sit upright, babies can hold on to an adult with their own body rather than having to be held. After about eight weeks, babies who are carried most of the time on their mothers' backs have to learn to cling and hold on when their mothers walk on rough ground, bend over in fields or stretch to pick fruit. This contrasts with the western practice of strapping babies into various kinds of baby seats, which encourages them to be passive.

The baby's ability to hold on is fundamental to many of the classic yoga postures adapted here for babies between 8 and 16 weeks. The postures are designed to accompany and enhance their overall development in accordance with yogic principles. They use flowing movements, which are better suited to babies than static postures. At this stage, babies love routine but hate monotony, so it is desirable to have continuity but with small variations in your yoga practice, introducing little games, rhymes and songs and, most of all, rhythm. As your baby gains greater co-ordination, yoga will invite her to discover the balance between calm and excitement that suits her.

Let your baby hold you

The idea of encouraging your baby to hold on to you may seem strange at first, since she still looks so small and vulnerable. This does not mean withdrawing support from your baby, but giving the appropriate minimal support at all times, to allow her to grow stronger and enjoy her body more. You can do this throughout the day, whenever your baby is awake. It will take several weeks of patient and careful initiative on your part, and some experimenting and strengthening on hers.

Sitting and kneeling

Whenever you sit on a firm bed or on the floor with your baby, you can sit her between your legs, her head and back against your body. If you wish, bring the soles of your feet together at first in the 'butterfly pose' to make a little enclosure for her. Gain the confidence not to hold her: the worst that can happen is that she will roll sideways on your thigh. If she does, pick her up and place her against you again. By doing this you are not trying to make your baby sit up before she is ready to do so. You are giving her back and head full support while also giving her a sense of freedom, to which she will become accustomed. As your baby becomes more familiar with yoga, you can sit her in the butterfly pose too. You are doing yoga together!

After gaining confidence in this sitting position, you can kneel on the floor and rest your baby on your knees against your body, if you find this position comfortable. Have your arms ready to hold your baby if she falls off to the side; this will rarely happen as she grows stronger. Your baby is learning to hold her unrestrained body against yours.

Standing and walking

You can also encourage your baby to hold you as you carry her when you are standing or walking. This may sound contradictory, because you have to hold her, but there are ways of holding a baby that enable her to hold you too. In western culture, we don't encourage our babies to hold on to our bodies as we move. As a result, they don't cling on, and have to be held tightly until they develop the conscious movements to hold on in their second half year or later. All babies can be taught actively to hold on more when they are carried, and the earlier you start, the better.

When you cradle your baby or hold her against you, relax your holding a little so that it still allows safe support but makes her aware of her body in relation to yours. The more relaxed your holding, the easier you make it for your baby to hold on to you as well as being held. At first she may respond with the reflex of opening her hands and then clinging to your clothes or hair. If you keep trying, as well as doing mini-drops (see page 39), you will give her physical incentives to take part in holding you when you hold her. This does not mean that you are withdrawing secure, comforting support; on the contrary, her active involvement will create greater closeness between you.

From safety position to hand support

Once you are confident with the safety position face-down and the extension of relaxed holding (see pages 36–7), you can use your flat hand only under your baby's chest. This will offer adequate support and greater freedom of movement. Try it carefully at first, over a soft surface. This position lets your baby's back stretch more, while your 'seat hand' offers support from below. You can use each hand alternately as the main support, swinging your baby back on your 'seat hand' and forth on your 'chest hand'. This swinging movement is the basis for all the balances that follow in this chapter.

Review of the basics

At each yoga session
• Be comfortable, aware of your body and in good spirits to 'set the mood';
• Have your baby lying comfortably on her back facing you, on your lap or on the bed or floor, between or in front of your legs;
• Always begin by making contact with your baby (see page 28), to show her that you are starting;
• Gradually increase the size, speed and pressure of your movements, taking cues from your baby to ensure that it is enjoyable for her.

Posture watchpoints
When doing standing poses, always have your

• Back straight

• Pelvis tilted slightly forward

• Knees slightly flexed

• Feet slightly apart

• Shoulders down

• Back of the neck elongated, chin down

The second hip sequence

This is a more energetic version of the first hip sequence for new babies on pages 32-3, with additional steps. Practicing it every day helps promote a healthy digestive system, relieving gas and constipation. This sequence also continues to open your baby's joints and increase their suppleness. It tones all the pelvic muscles in both the abdomen and the back.

Begin by making contact with your baby as described on page 28, and follow with full or dry massage, before doing the sequence.

1 Rolling knees

Holding your baby's bent knees together, roll them in a circle, to the left and then to the right, as close to the body as possible. Start with a small movement, increasing it as your baby gets used to it.

2 Acrobatic half lotus

As your baby's hip joints become more supple with practice, extend her foot slightly further to the opposite hip, and then toward her opposite armpit. If she is very supple, her foot can touch her nose or forehead.

Caution: never force this movement. Stop if you feel any resistance.

3 Butterfly

Bring the soles of your baby's feet together, opening her hips wide. Holding her feet with one hand, gently push them as close to her groin as possible.

Release the pressure, pull the feet toward you and repeat two or three times. You can also circle the feet around her hips in both directions to tone the lower back.

4 Closing the hips

After opening the hips, do the counterpose hip-closing movement described in the first hip sequence (no. 6 on page 34).

5 Push and counter-push

Now gently but firmly press the palms of your hands against the soles of your baby's feet. Release, and repeat. She may resist and push against your hands.

When you feel her responding, increase the pressure. You may also press on one foot at a time, which will encourage kicking.

6 Leg lift and drop

The sequence ends with this relaxing posture. It also shows your baby the use of the breath.

Holding a foot in each hand, gently lift her legs perpendicular to her body and then let them flop down relaxed. Inhale as you lift, and exhale as you let go.

Caution: don't lift your baby's hips off the floor until she seems ready for a bigger lift.

Twists

This sequence extends the twisting of the spine that you first practiced in a static way with your baby in the first hip sequence and are now doing as a circling movement in the second hip sequence. The twisting action affects the baby's whole spine, and helps open her chest and shoulders. In this sequence, synchronize your breathing with the movements you perform with your baby, and try to keep eye contact with her. Most babies find twists great fun, especially if you get into a lively rhythm.

Twists are a good preliminary to sequences for the upper body. They are essential for babies who have been reluctant to open out their arms since they were born, and invaluable if your baby prefers very gentle handling.

1 Spinal twist with massage

This full body twist and the stretch that follows combine well with massage. If you practice it with your baby naked you can massage the open side of her chest outward and extend your stroke into a shoulder and arm massage.

Caution: keep your baby's spine on the floor when you turn her legs sideways.

With your baby on her back as for the hip sequence, hold her bent knees together over her abdomen with your left hand. Take a breath and, exhaling slowly, bring your baby's knees to your left in a straight line.

At the same time, place your right hand flat on your baby's stomach and gently stroke it toward her left shoulder, pressing it open slightly with a light, brushing movement. Release the twist as you bring your hand back toward you without touching your baby.

Repeat this double action two or three times, paying attention to your breath. Repeat on the other side.

Take a short rest and have a stretch yourself after doing the spinal twist, staying in the same position.

2 Diagonal stretch

This stretch provides a lively counterpose to the deep action of the spinal twist.

Caution: take care that the back of her neck and head stay on the floor for this exercise, and that her spine is extended.

Take hold of your baby's right foot and left hand and bring them together, then open them out again diagonally, repeating a few times. At first, open without stretching to get your baby accustomed to the movement, then stretch out both her arm and her leg.

Repeat the same on the other side.

3 Binding

For a more supple or an older baby, try this extension of the diagonal stretch.

Bring your baby's right leg up along her left arm, so that her leg and arm are stretching in opposite directions. Cross and uncross your hands in this 'knotting' and opening up of your baby.

4 Brain gym circles

This more complex diagonal stretch not only tones the back muscles but also promotes good co-ordination of the limbs.

Holding your baby's opposite hand and leg in each hand, open them out slightly and circle them both inward a few times. Then circle them both outward.

Finally, circle her arm and leg in different directions and reverse the movement. It may take a few trials to get a smooth sequence, so it will test your co-ordination too.

Shoulder stand and roll

In the first and second hip sequences, you showed your baby the contrast between 'stretch' and 'relax' by gently extending her legs, raising them slightly to begin with and later lifting them vertically, and then letting them flop down. Now, with your baby in the same position, but on her back on your lap, between your legs or in front of you, you can introduce these more energetic contrasts.

First shoulder stand

This pose mirrors the inverted poses of yoga with a gentle, held shoulder stand, one of the most beneficial yoga postures.

Holding your baby's feet, raise her legs vertically until her bottom is lifted off the floor. Her head and shoulders remain on the floor while the rest of her body is raised with a stretch.

Hold on for a moment, looking at her, and then let her bottom and legs flop down softly. This becomes a first game of anticipation, particularly if you match it with a rising and falling voice, such as 'up, up, up, up... DOWN!'

Shoulder stand with a roll

If your baby enjoyed the shoulder stand, you can try extending it a little further.

Roll your baby's lifted legs over her head and then let her whole body unroll as you let her legs flop down.

Caution: if your baby finds this uncomfortable, wait until she is older for the full version of the pose.

Flying from the floor

Be guided by your baby's sense of fun during this rhythmical movement, and keep eye contact with her as much as possible. This exercise helps tone your abdominal muscles, while your baby, acting as a counterweight, enjoys the sensation of flying with the upswing of your legs.

1 Lying on your back with your knees folded close to the chest, place your baby on her stomach facing you. Holding her gently with your hands under her arms, lift her on to your bent knees, supporting her stretched body on your shins.

2 Holding your baby's hands or wrists, swing your legs rhythmically up and down, so that your baby feels herself 'flying'. At the same time your abdominal muscles are working, especially if you tuck in your chin and raise your head as you breathe out. Inhale and sit up smoothly, exhaling as you come up. Keep your baby in the same position against your legs.

Looping the loop

Holding a baby upside down looks dramatic, but is quite safe. Not only will your baby love it, but she will also receive all the benefits of the headstand, one of the main poses of Hatha yoga, which elongates the spine, increases the circulation to the brain, helps to clear the lungs of mucus and stimulates the whole nervous system. Follow the instructions carefully to get all the enjoyment this pose can bring to both of you. Doing a shoulder stand (page 52) is a good preparation for this inverted pose.

Once you are confident, you can 'loop the loop' in different positions, from back to front, front to back or side to side.

Caution
• If you have a specific concern about inverted poses for your baby, seek advice from your doctor.

• It is better not to practice this posture in front of people who are not familiar with yoga or with babies, as they may frighten your baby with expressions of fear. If this happens, comfort your baby first and then reassure them.

1 Lifting upside down

Sit on the floor or bed, or on an upright chair. Talk to your baby and make good eye contact, and then lay her prone on your lap.

Take her ankles, rather than her feet, firmly in both hands and in a sweeping movement lift her upside down with her back to you.

2 Holding and turning

Hold her high, turning your arms to one side so that you can see her face. If your baby is happy, give her a few seconds, up to a minute, to benefit from the inversion.

3 Coming down

To bring her down, prepare
to lay her carefully either
face-down or face-up on your
lap, whichever way feels more
comfortable. Land your baby on
her shoulders or on her chest
on your thigh, then drop her
feet gently until she lies prone
or on her back across your legs.

4 Resting

You can then roll her over on
your lap or between your legs.
Give her a moment to get her
bearings before you pick her up
and hug her.

Repeat the sequence two
or three times if your baby
is happy and wants more
excercise.

Caution
When lowering your
baby, take care to
place her shoulders
or chest, rather than
her head on your lap,
so as to avoid
any strain on
her neck.

Back stretches

Following the yogic principle of never forcing, it is always best to let babies under two months old increase their head and neck control spontaneously, rather than doing any stretching with them on their front. By her third month, however, your baby has probably started lifting up her head when lying on her front, as her back muscles get stronger and her spine begins to straighten. She will now be keen to extend her spine, arching her back to do so. This is a good time to begin back stretches.

The stretches on these pages stimulate the functioning of the digestive system, develop the baby's breathing and make her back strong as she begins to move independently.

Mini-cobra 1

For this classic yoga posture with your baby, sit with your back supported and your legs bent, and your baby lying prone along your thighs with her feet against your body and her head on or just beyond your knees. This is nice for smaller babies and makes your actions symmetrical. Alternatively, sit with her lying across one or both thighs. This is more conducive to a full relaxation of her back after stretching, but makes your action asymmetrical. An older baby can lie on the floor.

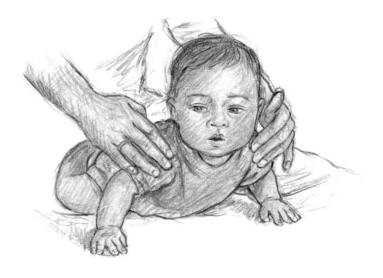

Start with massage strokes down your baby's spine. Then, holding your baby's rib cage in both hands under her chest, follow the intercostal muscles with your thumbs on each side of the spine, moving outward and exerting slight pressure. Proceed from the waist up to the upper back.

Then, with your thumbs just below your baby's shoulder blades, hold her shoulders and very gently bring them up, using your thumbs as levers. It does not matter whether your baby lifts her head or not at this stage.

Relax your hands and repeat two or three times.

Mini-cobra 2

With your baby lying transverse, place one hand on your baby's lumbar area and press it down gently but firmly. At the same time, slide your other hand under her breastbone with your index finger just below her chin.

Raise her chest slowly with your hand, maintaining the pressure on her back with your other hand.

Lower back stretch

Follow the mini-cobra with this stretch, in the same alternative positions but with your legs straighter. It is directed more specifically to the lower back, buttock and thigh muscles.

Holding your baby's ankles with one hand, place your other hand on her upper back, just below the shoulder blades, and stretch her legs toward you, lifting them slowly as far as seems comfortable. Let them flop back down as soon as you encounter resistance. Some babies lift their legs very little, others surprisingly high.

Caution: stop if you feel any resistance from your baby.

Counterpose

Counter these intense stretches with a bend. Bring your baby's knees to her chest while she is on her front, her side or her back, and rock her gently from side to side.

To follow what your baby is experiencing, try these two postures yourself, the cobra pose with your lower abdomen on the floor and the lower back stretch one leg at a time. Breathe as fully in your abdomen as you can.

Arm and shoulder stretches

These simple stretches open your baby's chest and expand her breathing. At the same time, they open your baby's trust. The lift stretch also intensifies the strengthening of the back muscles, which occurs before the baby can sit up. If you have practiced the twists on pages 50–1, your baby should have little if any resistance to these arm and shoulder stretches.

Caution: be careful never to force any movement.

Out stretch

With your baby on her back in front of you, hold her arms together at the wrists as you inhale. Exhaling slowly, stretch them out to her sides until you begin to feel resistance.

Bring back her arms, crossing them over each other twice on her chest, changing arms in the cross the second time. Repeat two or three times.

Circle stretch

In the same position as for the out stretch, hold your baby's wrists and gently bring them up over her face and open them out in a wide circle before coming back to centre again. Be attentive to the flow of your breath with the movement.

If your baby is happy to have her arms fully open, reverse the circling movement, lowering her arms before circling them up and bringing them back to centre on her chest.

Lift stretch

This stretch makes use of your baby's reflex grip to encourage her to hold on consciously and use her strength to lift herself up. Give your baby minimal support to do so, allowing her the pleasure of gaining further control of her body.

Lie on the floor with bent knees and sit your baby on your abdomen facing you. Place your index fingers in her hands; if she does not grip them, hold her hands in a relaxed way with your thumbs and index fingers.

Bring her arms to the sides of her head and lift her very gently, being aware of how she is using her muscles in her response.

If your baby is not yet strong enough to lift herself up, do not pull her up by the arms; instead, gently bring her down again. If she tries to lift herself,

allow her to do so before lowering her. Equally, if she lifts herself using your fingers as a lever, do not interfere, and offer her passive support as well as perhaps vocal encouragement.

Front crawl stretch

For this stretch, lie your baby prone and transverse on your legs, with her head resting on one of your thighs. Make it as active or as gentle as your baby requires it.

Hold her arms at the wrists and extend one arm up to the side and the other down alternately in a slow stretching movement. To make it more dynamic, do a 'front-crawl' action, which involves the shoulders to a greater extent.

More balances

As your baby grows and you handle her more confidently week by week, you can try some further balancing postures, which encourage her to hold on to you rather than being held. They also help her strengthen her back and legs in preparation for sitting, crawling and standing. Although babies change continually, at a given time your baby may be feeling cautious or rash; balances promote the 'middle path' between extremes – part of the philosophy of yoga – and the pleasure your baby takes in them will inspire you to do more.

Sitting banister hold

From the safety position face down, and progressing from holding your baby's arm to supporting her chest with your open hand (see pages 46–7), you can reduce support even more by offering her a 'banister rail' with your arm as she leans forward. This is the base position for a number of balancing poses.

First practise the 'banister hold' with your baby sitting sideways on your lap, with her legs to the outside of yours. With your arm as a 'banister', allow her to tip forward so that this is her only support. Then, using your other hand under her buttocks if needed, bring her back to a sitting position.

Repeat a few times. You can make it more fun with a verbal anticipation of the forward tipping with words such as 'sitting, sitting, GO!' or any others that come to you.

Try making a 'banister' for your baby as she sits on your lap facing away from you. With practice she becomes freer and freer to balance on your lap while you catch her with 'banisters' all around. This exercise promotes her sense of balance and helps her register the experience of going back to center.

See-saw

With your baby still sitting sideways on your lap, use one hand to support her chest on the front and the other to support the back of her head to create a see-saw movement of her body between your hands. Progress from a small to a wider movement, and allow more and more space between your hands and her body.

If she enjoys this, let her fall forward and backward and catch her just when it feels right.

Standing banister hold

Many babies like standing in a supported position from early on, long before they are ready to bounce on their legs. A banister hold will allow exactly as much support and as much freedom as your baby needs at the time.

Sit your baby sideways on your lap, with her feet on the floor or bed, using your arm on that side as a 'banister'. If she is keen to stand up, she will do so. Your other hand is ready to come to the rescue from the back and the 'banister' arm is taking most of her weight.

From balancing to flying

In these postures, your baby takes off in the air with your support. In the first three you have your hand – your seat hand – under her buttocks, in expansions of the seat hold and the banister hold for a younger baby (pages 38–9). Your baby will enjoy these more dynamic lifts, drops and swings as she gets older.

1 Seat balance

This pose encourages your baby to strengthen her spine from the base, and prepares her for the more dynamic moves that follow. Do it on a bed at first, for safety.

In a sitting or kneeling position, support your baby mainly with your seat hand under her buttocks while your other arm makes a 'banister rail' in front of her chest. Now release your 'banister' arm for a few seconds at a time, balancing your baby on your seat hand as she holds her back straight. As your baby and your supporting arm both become stronger, your banister arm will be more for protection than support.

2 Seat drops

Most babies like drops and are always ready for more. If these drops startle her, however, go back to the gentler mini-drops shown on page 39 and progress gradually back to these drops.

Balancing your baby on your seat hand, with your other hand supporting her back and neck, let her drop a little at first, gradually more, lowering your hands with a quick, crisp movement.

3 Seat lift

This movement, which can be combined with drops, will also strengthen your arms and tone your abdominal muscles. Use breath awareness to help you with this pose.

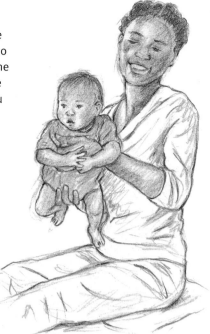

With your seat hand under your baby's buttocks and your other hand supporting her chest, lift her up in the air with a sideways shoving movement.

Repeat two or three times if your baby enjoys it.

4 First flier

This is a favourite with dads because of the simple action. It acts as a useful toner of the abdominal muscles, but you need to be quite strong to do it.

Lie on the floor with your knees bent and your baby sitting facing you on your abdomen. Pick her up firmly under the arms and 'fly' her forward until she is hovering above you and looking down at you.

Standing swings, drops and lifts

Once your baby no longer needs head support, all the drops, lifts and swings that you have practiced sitting down or kneeling can now be done standing. If your baby enjoyed the mini-drop and mini-swing shown on page 39, she will love these more energetic versions. You can do these bigger movements in the same position facing away from you, or as shown here.

Side swing

With your baby in the cradling seat hold position, her head resting on your left arm if you are right-handed, progress gradually from a gentle rocking movement to a swing, stopping briefly when you get to the end of the movement on each side. If your baby is becoming too heavy for this position, it may be easier to do it with her facing away from you.

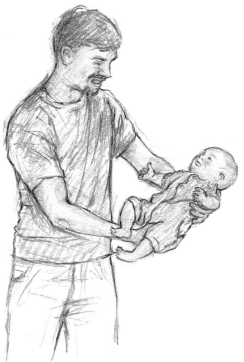

Big swing

If your baby shows her delight with swinging, move on to a wider swing with your arms extended.

Hold her as before, but with your cradling arm round her shoulder and her arm between your thumb and index finger to provide additional security. In the big swing, your baby will be head down either on the way up or on the way down, according to how you hold her.

Tailor the swings to your baby's reactions, always moving very gradually from a small movement to a wider one.

Caution: avoid any shaking or jostling movements and make sure your baby's head is well supported on your arm across her chest.

Standing drop

This movement corresponds to the more dynamic practice of Hatha yoga. Many fathers especially enjoy handling their baby in this way, once she has gained head and neck control.

Bend your knees slightly and relax your shoulders as you pick up your baby, holding her firmly on the sides of her rib cage. Take a breath in and lift her up to face your chest, then let her drop gently, relaxing your arms as you exhale.

When she is used to this drop, lift her up higher so that she is face to face with you, for a bigger drop.

Caution: if your baby does not have full head control yet it is better to postpone these two excercises until later.

Standing lift

You can add rhythm and height to the standing drop to make it a standing lift, expanding the flow of your breath in the movement.

Breathe in, and lift your baby upright as high as your arms allow. Let her drop down as you breathe out. Resist bringing your baby high above your head; keep her body upright throughout the lift and the drop.

Walking relaxation

In contrast with the first relaxation, described on pages 42–3, in which you cradled your baby or lay down with her resting on your body, this relaxation is done while walking with your baby. You will still find the other positions useful; indeed, as your baby grows, you may find increasing benefit from regularly lying down for relaxation with her. Walking relaxation is an additional, less conventional, but very effective way of relaxing, especially with a younger, lighter baby. Done if possible out of doors every day, it can greatly reduce any tension or depression you may be feeling, and increase your sense of well-being.

1 Release tension

Release tension from your whole body, ideally before picking up your baby, by 'wobbling', shaking yourself loose all over. Relax your lower jaw as you do this and 'blow raspberries' to make sure that you have done it. An older baby will find this very funny.

2 Grounding

With your baby in the 'relaxed holding' face-down position (page 36), do a few gentle drops with her, accompanying the movement. This 'grounds' both of you and prepares you and your baby for the steps that follow.

3 Your position

Hold your baby in a comfortable walking position that gives you close contact with her, such as relaxed or upright holding.

4 The first step

Set your intent on a rhythmical movement, an unfolding of your action in space and time, which is the essence of each yoga sequence. This will help you empty your mind of all its current preoccupations. Concentrate on your first step.

5 Start walking

Take a step and start walking slowly, checking the alignment of your spine in relation to your pelvis as you walk, and the way you place your feet on the ground.

6 Breathing

Now pay attention to your breathing. Exhale to help release residual tension, a few times if necessary. Yawn if you wish, then inhale for two steps. Lengthening each exhalation slightly helps you take in more air in your next breath without forcing your breathing.

7 Awareness

Feel your baby's body against yours and be aware of your two bodies in the rhythm of your walking. While being superficially attentive to the placing of your feet and to your surroundings, 'empty your gaze', looking both outward and inward. Turn your attention to the flow of the universal life force in your two joined selves.

Yoga with action rhymes

By now you may have already got a repertoire of songs that you sing when you do yoga with your baby. The nursery rhymes of your childhood may have come back to you, prompted by your baby. If not, many recordings made for toddlers and small children will delight young babies too, particularly if you transform them into action songs with yoga. The more you animate yoga with singing, the more you promote the kind of communication that stimulates all your baby's senses and involves her in the 'spiral of joy'.

The following two traditional nursery rhymes and a dance rhyme offer examples of how you can match the yoga postures you have practiced with your baby to songs. You can also create your own action rhymes with any other tunes you know and like.

Row your boat

You can match this rhyme to a gentle arm stretch from early on, as your baby comes to enjoy opening her chest out more with yoga. At first you can have your baby lying on your bent knees facing you as you sit with your back supported. Later your baby may be on her back on the floor between your open legs as you sit, and then sitting up as shown on page 105. It is satisfying for your baby that you also take part in the action so that this can be a joint practice.

You can also do this with another parent and baby, as shown below. If you are able to sit unsupported with your legs straight, it can involve you in the most classic of forward bends in Hatha yoga, which has a wide range of physical and other benefits.

'Baby yoga gives me something fun and purposeful to do with Finn at times of the day when he and I are tired or cranky. A yoga session always leaves us feeling happier and much more in tune with each other than we were before.'

Row, row, row your boat,
Gently down the stream;
(alternate forward bends, breathing in on the way back, out into the bend)

Merrily, merrily, merrily, merrily,
(arms in the air)

Life is but a dream.
(let yourself go all the way back with your baby leaning on you)

Wind the bobbin up

Your baby will enjoy the actions of this rhyme passively at first, and then participate more and more actively as her co-ordination increases. It is a dynamic sequence that will stimulate all your baby's developing senses in a way that is both repetitive and varied, with a marked contrast between stretching and relaxing movements. It may help her forget a discomfort or upset in a few seconds.

Do this with your baby sitting against you, in your lap or between your knees. Hold her hands and guide them through the rhyme.

Wind the bobbin up,
Wind the bobbin up ,
(winding movement)

Pull, pull,
(pull arms open)

Clap, clap, clap.
(hands together to clap)

(repeat)

Point to the ceiling,
(one hand up)

Point to the floor,
(one hand down)

Point to the window,
(one hand right)

Point to the door.
(one hand left)

Wind the bobbin up,
(winding movement, and as above)

Wind the bobbin up,

Pull, pull,

CLAP, CLAP, CLAP!
(with a stronger finale)

Hokey cokey/Hokey pokey

This dance rhyme involves your baby's whole body. It is open ended and, although only the first stanza for the leg action is given here, use the same movements with the arms and finish with a very energetic 'whole self' in and out. You can also play with the rhythm. With older babies, it is especially effective if you increase the tempo so that as you repeat the sequence the movements become faster and faster. Doing the hokey cokey is excellent for rainy or cold days when taking your baby out may not be possible, or whenever you both need some lively distraction.

It is best done in a sitting position, as for 'Wind the bobbin up', but can be adapted to any position you find comfortable. When you get to the chorus, if you are strong and energetic enough, lifting your baby above your head, as shown, will add to your baby's enjoyment.

You put your right foot in,
Your right foot out,
In, out, in, out,
Shake it all about,
You do the hokey cokey
And you turn around,
And that's what it's all about!

Oooh, the hokey cokey,
Oooh, the hokey cokey,
Oooh, the hokey cokey,
Knees bent,
Arms stretched,
Ra Ra Ra!

You put your left foot in... etc.

Games with yoga

It is often not until they have their second child, and watch her interacting with her older brother or sister, that parents realize that even very young babies love playing games. If we engage babies in play from early on, they soon seem to know that it is different from any other activity. Introducing an element of play into baby yoga will confirm to your baby (in a physical way different from feeding) that life is enjoyable.

Ball games

Balls are probably the most ancient toy of all. All babies like balls and balloons, and 'ball' is often the first object they name. Playing with balls can involve your family and friends with your baby and introduce variety to your yoga session. Sit in a circle or, if there are two adults, make a diamond shape with your legs to enclose her. Small soft balls cannot hurt your baby and she will enjoy watching you play with them at first. Soon she will be able to grab hold of them as her eye-to-hand co-ordination is stimulated through watching and getting involved in as many games as you can think of (for example, mini-soccer).

4 Fun and growth

Since he was born, you have played with your baby and enjoyed each achievement with him, however small. Yoga has helped your baby grow strong, supple and balanced, as well as enabling him to communicate more fully with you, making use of all his senses. Now the range of his responses is changing; he is both guiding you and expecting your guidance on which experiences will give him most pleasure and satisfaction as he grows.

Your baby can now reach and grasp objects. Rattles and soft toys amuse him, but his own hands and feet are just as fascinating. Playing with them, putting them in his mouth, and moving them as he chooses give him an increasing sense of his power to make things happen around him. Faces and expressions, and yours most of all as his parent, continue to be a favourite source of games, in which he wants to be more and more involved. He is taking advantage of all the opportunities presented to him to develop, through play, the skills he needs to grow.

Together you can develop your yoga practice in ways that suit you both, perhaps with more energetic physical play and high lifts or tossing in the air, or with more songs and action rhymes, or with long cuddly relaxations, or with all these combined. While some babies will continue to enjoy doing yoga lying on their back well after they are able to sit and crawl, others will assert their independence and prefer to develop their own more active games with yoga.

At this stage, as he gains full control of his movements and begins to discover and enjoy the world around him, fun and growth are what your baby strives for. A short daily yoga practice offers this, as you now give your baby minimal yet effective support in each posture, while being an ever-appreciative witness of his progress.

Resuming or developing your own yoga practice at this stage will also have an effect on your growing baby. Ideally, combine your own postures with his in a joint daily practice that may be your first shared activity besides swimming. He may want to imitate you and join in, as you use your body for your own fun and growth too.

Energy, rhythm and fun

Sometime between his fifth and seventh month, your baby will give you signs that he is ready for something different. He will start to take charge of the yoga sequence on the floor, grabbing his feet or rolling over, or both, and showing you 'his' yoga. It is the inevitable result of you having given him more and more incentives to stretch, lift, push and pull himself up as much as his strength has allowed at each stage of his development.

As your baby begins to explore the world, using his newly acquired skills to do so, you need to adapt and change your yoga practice with him. Your practice will not be substantially different but its mood and purpose will be; yoga is now helping your baby to grow into his physical autonomy and individuality. He still needs to feel secure and close to you throughout this process. He trusts that you acknowledge and back up his efforts, that you comfort him in his frustration and rejoice with him in his victories.

Let your baby set the mood

Earlier, when you 'set the mood' for your mutual enjoyment of yoga (see pages 26–7) it was mainly to make sure your baby was receptive. Now you can let him take the lead, simply 'making space' for him to set the mood for his own fun and growth. (If your baby is more than five months old when you begin to do yoga, this is a good starting point.) The following simple meditative practice may help you enjoy the transition.

• Before touching your baby or taking hold of his feet, sit or kneel back as he lies on his back in front of you in your usual starting position for the hip sequence.

• Watch your baby, making eye contact with him if possible. You may choose to talk to him or to remain silent. You can also center yourself with the techniques described on pages 16-17.

• Mentally, make space for your growing child, acknowledging that he is not a young baby any longer and will be detaching from you more. If you feel sad or anxious about this, own these feelings.

• Register what your baby is doing. He may be practicing his latest skill, such as turning over or raising his hips, or clamoring for

your attention if you went deep into your feelings.

• Respond to your baby both verbally and with a simple posture such as 'stretch–relax', lifting and stretching his legs as you inhale, letting them flop as you exhale.

• Have a good stretch in front of your baby, breathing deeply.

Rhythms

As your baby grows and spends more time awake, he needs to ex-perience a greater contrast between activity and rest, stretching and relaxing, being awake and being asleep. Yoga offers your baby a heightened version of these contrasts and stimulates his biorhythms so that he will be more active when awake and will also sleep better and more deeply. After 16 weeks, introducing more definite and dynamic rhythms into the yoga postures will appeal to him. You can make them strong and striking or light and subtle, to suit your baby's current preference. Whenever there is rhythm, there is play, and your baby will find himself drawn happily into the postures.

Invite, never force

As your baby is now stronger and strives to lift himself from the floor, you may be tempted to complete his movements by lifting him or pushing him further in particular postures. It is important, however, to invite – but never force – your baby's movements after 16 weeks. By continuing to offer minimal but effective support, you give your baby the message that he is 'in charge' and that this is fun and safe because you are there to support and guide him.

'I only started practicing yoga when pregnant and I fully intend to continue doing so. Through baby yoga I gained confidence in handling my son and learned how to physically play with him rather than just jiggling him up and down and shaking toys in his face.'

The third hip sequence

This hip sequence is more energetic than the previous two (pages 32–3 and 48–9), and with a faster rhythm that marks the full extension of the movements. Introduce the change of rhythm gradually, or whenever you feel your baby will welcome it. The sequence also adds three new steps: binding, an extended twist and a mini-plough. Make the sequence more dynamic by doing the steps without pausing, and by creating a clearer contrast between stretching and relaxing, action and rest. As with all hip sequences, make contact with your baby and do massage before you start.

If your baby no longer seems to enjoy lying on his back for yoga, practice it with him sitting on your lap with his back against you. It is more effective when he lies on his back, however, so after a few days try returning to this position. He may welcome it after the brief change.

1 Knees to chest

See page 32. Do this several times, pressing the knees against the sides of his abdomen and releasing them.

2 Rolling knees

See page 48. Circle your baby's knees together, close to his body, several times in each direction.

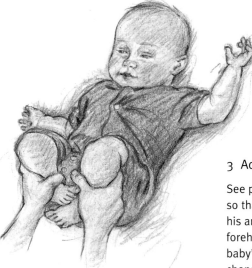

3 Acrobatic half lotus

See page 48. Extend this pose so that your baby's feet reach his armpits, shoulders, nose or forehead. Clap the soles of your baby's feet together before changing side each time, getting into a steady rhythm.

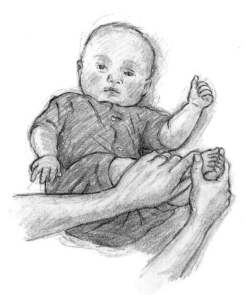

4 Extended twist

This develops the spinal twist with massage on page 50, but you now bend the knees first, then hold the legs straight.

5 Binding

Develop the binding shown on page 51 by making it more rhythmical and extending the foot and arm farther on each side.

6 Butterfly

See also page 49. This time do all the movements, first pressing your baby's feet on his perineum, then out, then up, then circling them in a lively rhythm.

7 Closing the hips

See page 33. As you repeat the joining and drawing in movement of your baby's hips, make a wider circle with the knees, opening the hips further.

8 Push and counter-push

See also page 49. Press your palms against the soles of your baby's feet, first together and then alternately, encouraging stronger resistance from your baby.

9 Mini-plough

This extends the stretching and relaxing of the leg lift and drop on page 49. You now push your baby's lifted legs over his head and gently release, letting his whole body unroll to the floor.

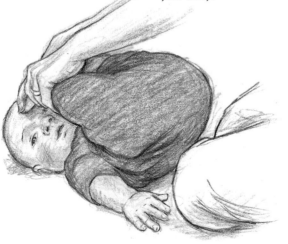

The roller-coaster

This stretch sequence is a more dynamic and expanded version of the back stretches on pages 56–7. Your legs become a 'roller coaster' for a ride that can be as hair-raising or as gentle as your baby likes it, and that offers you both a great deal of exercise as well as fun. The sequence also helps prepare your baby for crawling and climbing.

Caution: adapt the movements to your baby's taste and your ability. If you go too high or too vigorously for him, stop and cuddle him.

1 Start gently

Sit comfortably on the floor, on a cushion if needed. Place your baby on his front across your extended legs. Make sure he is relaxed, and perhaps give him a brief back massage.

Take your legs a short distance apart to stretch your baby's back. Then bend one knee, raising and stretching your baby's upper body while keeping your other leg on the floor. Bend and straighten alternate knees, to lower his upper body and lift his buttocks and legs with a stretch. Make the movement rhythmical, like a see-saw.

2 Stretch and bend

Opening your legs slightly more to stretch your baby, hold his ankles with your hands. Pull and lift his legs straight and then bend them to the sides of his body, still holding his legs. Stretch and bend several times in a pleasant rhythm.

Vary the movement by stretching one leg and bending the other. Be careful not to push your baby forward. Make your movement light, stretching and bending the legs only from the hips.

3 Rolling...

With your knees slightly bent at the same height, roll them anticlockwise if your baby's head is to your left, clockwise if it is to your right. Straighten your legs as they reach the floor in a 'roller-coaster'-like movement, which will also tone your abdominal muscles. Play games with the motion by going one way, reversing, starting again, going fast and slowly.

If your baby loves stretching his whole body across your legs, let him do so before continuing.

4 ...and unrolling

After a short rest, continue rolling, this time down and back up your legs.

With your legs flat on the floor, place your hands on your baby and push him gently so that he rolls over along your legs. Then 'unroll' him back to the starting position. Your baby will soon learn to relax completely throughout the movement, as he grasps that the more floppy he is, the better he rolls and the more fun it is.

At each session roll him farther down your legs, unrolling him until he is back on your lap. If you are energetic, raise him in your arms for a kiss before rolling him again.

Lifts, slides and rolls

Once your baby is used to going upside down (see pages 54–5), you can make the movement more dynamic by combining it with forward and backward slides and rolls on your body. If your baby still wants more, add the rest of the exercises shown on these pages, or your own variations, for an even more energetic and acrobatic sequence.
Caution: as with all upside-down postures, take great care not to strain your baby's neck when you lower him back on to your legs.

1 Lift and slide

Repeated a few times, this posture becomes a game in which your baby anticipates that you will grab hold of his ankles again after he lands on your legs.

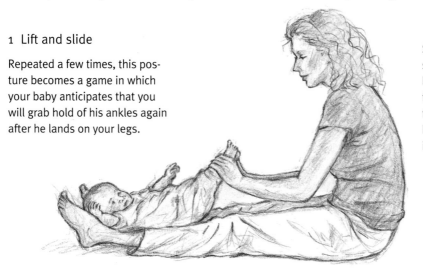

Sitting up with your legs straight out, have your baby lying on or between your legs facing you. Holding his ankles firmly with both hands, slide him toward you and lift him up in the air.

Lower your baby down so that he rests on his front along your legs, and when he lifts his head he is facing you. Hold his ankles again, slide him away from you and lift him upside down as before.

Land him on your legs again, this time on his back with his feet toward you.

Repeat this sequence several
times if your baby enjoys it, and
watch him stretch out to find
you there as he lands on your
legs from the inversion.

2 Flying from the floor

See page 53. From this
position, lie down on your
back with your bent legs in
the air and your baby on
board, and 'fly from the floor'.

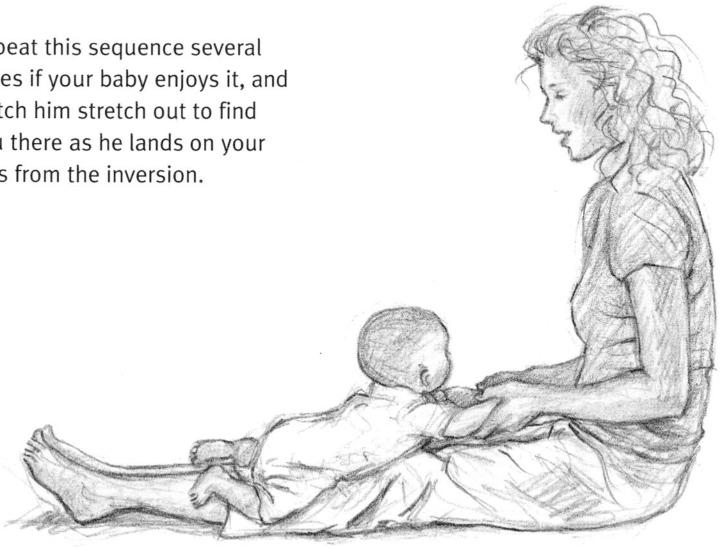

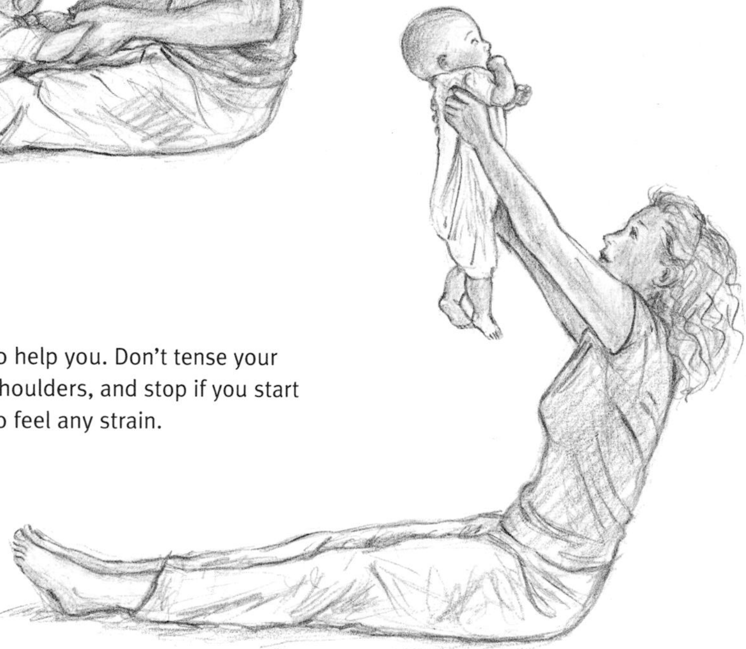

3 Acrobatic lift

This is also a good exercise for
strengthening your abdominal
and lower back muscles.

Take your baby firmly under
the arms and in a sweeping
movement lift him into the air.
Hold the position for a few
seconds, using your breathing

to help you. Don't tense your
shoulders, and stop if you start
to feel any strain.

4 Rolling over

As you bring your baby down
until he is sitting then lying
on your legs as before, make
use of the momentum to roll
his legs over his head. Make
it a small roll or a mini-plough
(see page 77), as your
baby prefers.

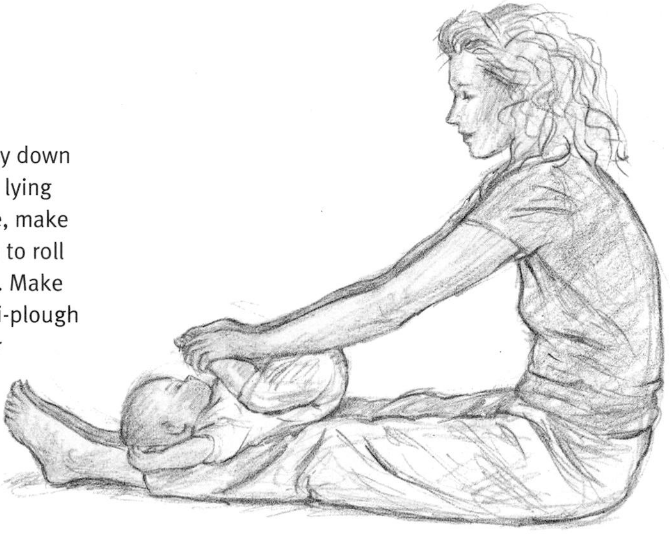

Self-lifts

Since your baby was about two months old, you have been letting him hold you, rather than holding him (see pages 46–7). You have felt his muscle tone gradually increase, to the point when he grabs hold of your clothes or any part of you he can, in order to pull himself up. Now he is likely to take the hint of minimal support – one finger or a hand to guard his back – and raise himself into a sitting and then a standing position. In this exercise you are merely offering support until you can share the triumph of his breakthrough, his enjoyment of doing it 'all by himself'.

From lying down

With your baby lying down in front of you when you are sitting or kneeling, for example at the end of the hip sequence, give him a hint to lift himself up to a sitting position by placing your index fingers in his hands. If you started yoga with him early, he may sit up straight away.

Caution: do not lift your baby up by the arms, but let him find his own strength to lift himself up. The movement is only prompted by you; it is initiated and controlled by your baby.

You can help your baby lift himself up when you are sitting down. Sit with your legs apart in front of you and your baby lying on the floor in between. Extend your arms out in front of you, bending them at the elbow, and give your baby two fingers to hold. He may use this support to bring himself up, if he is ready to do so. If not, try again after a few days. Your baby may be content to sit up and immediately get interested in what's going on around him once he is comfortable. Let him do this, maintaining minimal support. He may fall back if he gets distracted or tired and relaxes his back muscles. Be relaxed enough in your holding to let him go down, your fingers still in his hands, rather than react by pulling him up. Always lower your baby gently when he relaxes his back muscles, following his own movement.

If your baby can't wait to stand up, don't frustrate him by expecting him to sit first. Give him time to stretch, as he may need to flex his legs a few times before mustering the strength he needs to lift himself up all the way. Then enjoy his triumphant smile. Allow him to flop back to a sitting position when he gets tired, which may be after only a couple of seconds at first, and then to lie down again.

Caution: once he has succeeded in sitting or standing up, your baby may want to do so again and again, until he is frustrated and exhausted. Knowing when to stop is important, to avoid overstimulation. Take your baby in your arms and move on to something completely different, such as swings.

From kneeling

If your baby lands on his knees against your leg after a posture such as the upside-down sequence, you can offer him your index fingers to encourage him to lift himself up. If he is ready to do so, he will enjoy this opportunity to stretch in a different way.

From balances

Sit with your baby sitting sideways on one leg, facing outward. Let him balance back and forth as shown on pages 60–1. If your baby is steady, and his feet can touch the floor in the forward movement, give him your index fingers to hold and gently increase the swing. He may welcome the opportunity to stretch himself into a standing position, before dropping back to sitting and reclined positions as you continue the balances.

If twisting your body sideways to give your baby a finger hold is uncomfortable, your baby can practice standing holding on to your fingers from any sitting position, such as on your lap facing away from you, as shown. Some babies like to stretch further on to their tiptoes and find a rocking movement of their own that will help strengthen their lower back even more.

Flying: higher lifts and drops

When your baby has full control of his neck and greater command of his whole body, you can safely increase the height of the lifts and drops from a sitting or kneeling position. This is the time when your baby will begin to enjoy being thrown up in the air. If as a father you were disappointed that your baby cried when you tried to do this earlier, do it again 'the yoga way' and you may be surprised at how high your baby likes to go. As your baby grows heavier, the arm of your 'seat hand' has to get stronger. Kneeling is easier than sitting when doing these lifts, but there will come a time when you need to stand to do them (see pages 92–3).

Caution: balancing your baby on your seat hand can feel like an 'egg and spoon' race at first so, until you feel confident, practice over a bed or cushions. It is, however, a steady hold in which you feel the full strength of your baby's back muscles.

Facing foward

These lifts rapidly strengthen your baby's back enough for you to be able to hold him upright using only your 'seat hand', with your other hand ready to offer backup support if need be.

With your strong hand as 'seat hand' and your other hand as support under your baby's chest, hold him upright and, gaining momentum with your arms, lift him up in the air, catching him as he comes down with your hands still in the same position. At first, make it a very small lift with just a small gap between his body and your hands. As you gain experience – and strength – gradually lift him higher and catch him as he comes down.

Up facing you

Hold your baby firmly under his arms facing you, and lift him up in the air above your head if you can. Inhale before you lift and exhale as you are lifting.

Then, if you wish, place him on your head, face down. The pressure of his abdomen on your head may make him giggle, or he may grab hold of your hair.

Caution: lifting with the breath helps you avoid straining your lower back in a sitting position.

Up facing away from you

Hold your baby firmly under his arms facing away from you, and lift him up in the air above your head if you can. Inhale before you lift and exhale as you are lifting. Sit him on one of your shoulders, or on your head, before lowering him down to sit between your legs.

Bigger balances

Before your baby can sit or stand by himself, balances will help him retain his centre of gravity as he learns to distribute his weight in different positions. By balancing within the security of your arms, he learns to stay relaxed and not mind losing his balance for a moment, since he knows that he will find it again in another way. Balances for babies over four months old allow for greater movement than the earlier ones for younger babies, and let your baby enjoy playing with safe risk. He knows that you are always there to catch him, and he can let himself fall. You initiate and control the movement while your baby responds passively and learns to relax in the movement itself.

From sitting to standing

These exercises will help your baby enjoy the transition toward taking all his weight on his feet, and will increase his self-control and awareness of risk later on.

Sitting balances

Sit or kneel comfortably with your baby. With one arm in a 'banister' position (see page 60) across his chest, use your other, seat hand to sit him sideways on one of your legs. Use your arms to push your baby gently in all directions, keeping him from falling in whichever direction he moves. Let your baby roll back on your legs before sending him forward again.

If your baby comes to stand up at the end of his forward movement, you can let him lift himself as described on pages 82–3. Your baby may also get into a kneeling position at the end of his forward movement, especially if he is not yet strong enough to lift himself up into a standing position. This can become a lively game, in which your baby enjoys falling backward as much as leaning forward.

Balances and drops

Gradually your baby will develop enough strength in his back to balance by himself, and will use his feet to push himself forward on to your banister arm from the floor, before dropping back on to your lap. Encourage his trials verbally while he relies on your arm support for security. For a balance with a drop, don't use your seat hand to support your baby from behind. Only your banister arm or hand, in the same position as before, protects him from falling forward, while he drops back on to your lap.

When your baby has developed skill at balancing and his back is strong enough, you could do a 'big drop', in which you let him find his balance while you hold only his hands.

- Bend your knees up and sit your baby on them, holding his hands. Take a breath and drop your legs to the floor as you exhale, surprising your baby with a gentle or steep 'big drop', depending on his age and temperament. (You can add action rhymes for this, such as 'This is the way the gentleman rides'.)

Standing balances

When your baby is almost ready to stand by himself, you can let him do a sitting to standing balance.

- Sit him on your knees with his feet on the floor. With your hand across his chest, let him go forward and find his balance in a standing position, leaning slightly forward.

- To bring him back to sitting on your knees, press your arm gently on his chest.

When your baby is more confident about standing, you can help him balance in this position with a swing. Each time he pushes forward on to your banister arm, push him gently back, still standing, on to your seat hand with a swinging movement.

Picking up your baby with yoga

As your baby gets heavier, protecting your lower back as you pick him up becomes a priority. The way you pick up your baby is important for him too: he needs to feel unrestricted. If you make picking him up fun and freeing for him, it will remind him – and you – that yoga applies to all movements throughout the day. To tone your abdominal muscles and make it even more fun for your baby, combine picking him up with a lift, extending your arms and lifting him above your head.

Squat and lift
You don't have to be able to sustain a squat to squat and lift your baby in one movement. Practice it without a baby at first. This can become an enjoyable stretch each time you pick up your baby, and your back will adjust to his increasing weight.

- Before you start, lengthen your spine by extending your arms above your head while bending your knees, keeping your back straight as if you were going to sit on an imaginary stool.

- Then lower your arms and swing them back up as you straighten your legs. Standing with your feet apart, you can now bend your knees and scoop your baby with a similar movement, holding him firmly under the arms. Use the end of your exhalation to pick him up before starting your in-breath in the lifting movement itself.

Arm roll in safety position
This way of picking up a baby from the floor uses the safety position that you have practiced since your baby's earliest weeks. Now you can make it more dynamic and fun for your baby as well as easier for you as your baby gets heavier. It is also the least disturbing way of lifting a sleeping baby.

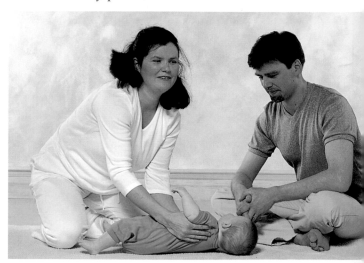

- Bend your knees, with your feet wider than your hips for balance, or start from a kneeling position. Slide your supporting arm under your baby, and then, if he was supine on the floor, roll him over on to this arm with your seat hand, so that he faces down on your arm.

- Placing your seat hand under his bottom, you can now straighten your legs (or go into a kneeling lift – see below) and bring him up safely, with minimal strain on your lower back and minimum handling of your baby.

Swing and lift

A standing forward bend is a good way to lift a baby from the floor if your knees are stiff. Practice lifting your baby in this way from both sides to avoid straining the back.

- Take a wide step along one side of your baby. Bend your back leg slightly and swing your arms a few times to feel the movement you are going to make.

- The next time you swing backward, stretch to pick up your baby with both hands under his arms as you swing forward, extending your back leg and now bending your front leg in the lift. Start lifting at the end of your exhalation as you move back, and inhale fully in the lift itself.

Getting up together

This is easier than it looks, particularly with a baby heavy enough to provide a good counterweight. Doing the movement daily will help increase your strength and suppleness.

- Sit on the floor with your knees bent and feet flat, holding your baby under his arms in front of you, facing you at first and later in any position. Move your center of gravity forward as you inhale and, holding your baby away from you, lift yourself up with him.

Kneeling lift

This stable, steady way to pick up your baby is an adapted kneeling warrior pose in two steps. The more you breathe abdominally in this movement, the lighter and more effortless it becomes.

- Kneeling upright in front of your baby, bring one foot forward to one side of him so that your foot is perpendicular to your knee. Put your hands under his arms and sit him on your raised knee, facing you if he was on his back, away from you if he was on his front.

- Inhale and move your centre of gravity forward. Lower your buttocks as much as you can, pressing on your front foot, and come up holding your baby as you exhale. It helps at first to turn the toes of your back foot under to come up.

Relaxed holding with a heavier baby

Holding your baby in a relaxed way (see also pages 36–7) not only protects your back but also feels more comfortable, and your baby will sense your ease and greater stability as you carry him. Modify the way you hold your baby at regular intervals as his weight increases, checking his position on your body (see box below) and adjusting slings or carriers accordingly.

Adapting the safety position

A variation of the safety position when your supporting arm feels tired, or you want to keep one hand free, is to rest your baby's buttocks on your hipbone. It's a better alternative to the more common habit of sitting a baby astride the hips, which may cause pelvic asymmetry and lead to long-term problems with posture and walking. It is much more comfortable to use your hipbone as a support, and it also acts as a substitute for your seat hand in the safety position.

- Sit your baby against your hipbone, facing outward, with your arm across his chest on the same side. In this way you can walk freely and reach out with your other hand, and your baby has a good view of the world. Relax your shoulder as much as possible so that your arm is a 'banister' and your baby rests mainly on your hipbone.

Check your position

For maximum freedom of movement while holding your baby in a relaxed way, you need to find your center of gravity together. To do this, hold him against you on your front, either facing you or facing away from you as is most comfortable. Now lower him with both hands under his arms from your upper chest to your lower abdomen in a relaxed, slow movement. Do this several times, exhaling as the baby moves down your body, and try to notice which points in the movement feel best. When you have spotted one or two points, hold your baby there and try the following checks:

- Do you feel free to bend your knees with your back straight?

- Can you breathe freely with your chest wide open?

- Can you move your arms and legs – one at a time – while holding your baby comfortably in a relaxed way in this position?

If you are fit, see if you can lift one leg up straight. Try relaxing your arms and shoulders one at a time to make sure you are not accumulating any unsuspected tension there. Flop and shake your hands (which may amuse your baby).

Firefighter's hold with arm support

Carrying your baby relaxed in this way is a development of the upright relaxed holding on your shoulder for younger babies, shown on page 40. It may take a few tries before your baby relaxes in this position if you did not practice it when he was younger, but he will eventually associate it with relaxed holding, particularly if you walk with him in this way. You can use it throughout your baby's growth into a small child, even up the age of six.

- Place your baby's chest on your shoulder with his arms hanging down your back so that if he wishes he can relax his head completely over your shoulder and feel balanced as you carry him.

- You can provide additional support with your arm on the same side under his seat, although you may find that it is hardly needed since your shoulder should be taking all your baby's weight.

The 'floppy' underarm position

This position may be useful on walks, when your baby might also find it relaxing and conducive to sleep. It is also a good position to use when you feel anxious or tense, in order to avoid conveying negative emotion to your baby through tight holding. If you breathe deeply as you walk with him, you may find that diffusing the emotion is easier.

- From the safety position, on your hipbone or not, slide your baby to your waist so that he lies prone with your arm around his back and chest. In this position many babies go 'floppy', particularly if they are less than six months old.

- Try skipping and relaxed jogging (see also the stretching walks described on pages 94–5) while carrying your baby 'floppy' under your arm, and watch his reactions.

Caution: if your baby's neck is not strong yet, it is best to use the 'floppy' underarm position for relaxed walking only.

From high lifts to low drops

When your baby is familiar with lifts and drops from a sitting or kneeling position, you can practice high lifts and low drops in a standing position. Starting and ending with relaxed holding and progressing gradually from small to wider movements, you will gain strength and balance in the way you handle him. With all these postures, either use both hands to lift and receive your baby firmly or use your seat hand as the main support and your chest hand to give additional support. If you decide that these high lifts are not for you or him, choose other yoga poses with your baby that you both enjoy.

Seat lift with low drop

Hold your baby in the safety position, your seat hand supporting his upright back from the buttocks. Loosely rest your supporting hand under your baby's chest.

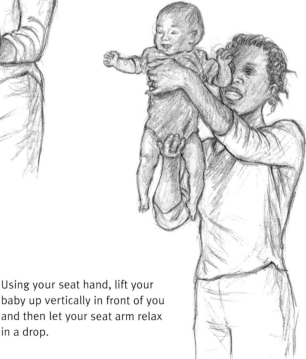

Using your seat hand, lift your baby up vertically in front of you and then let your seat arm relax in a drop.

Raising baby, low drop

This is a standing version of the high lift shown on page 85, and can be transformed into a throw when your baby is ready.

Caution: if you raise your baby quite high, bend your knees slightly and don't lean back.

High throws

Most babies find high throws exhilarating, but don't do more than two or three at once, since they can be overstimulating.

From the seat lift (see page 92), add a throw by releasing your supporting hand as you lift your baby and throwing him up in the air from the base of your seat hand, catching him with both hands as he comes down again.

Caution: stand steady to receive him, as his weight may surprise you when he comes down.

Weightlifting with your baby

The deep breathing in this held position makes it a yoga pose rather than just 'weightlifting' with your baby. As you involve your abdominal muscles in your breathing, all your body's systems are stimulated.

For stability, step one foot forward. With your baby resting on your head, face down or up, hold the sides of his chest firmly and lift him straight up, extending your arms as you inhale and continuing to stretch as you exhale. As you stretch up your baby is also stretched.

Continue breathing as deeply as possible, before lowering him gently.

Stretching walks

The more you practice yoga with your baby, the more he will get into a relaxed mode, while increasingly holding on to you when you carry him. Stretching walks combine physical stimulation for your baby with exercise for you that strengthens the muscles of your lower back, legs and arms. Using your breathing consciously as you walk will enhance your enjoyment, and can be done as a sequence in which you both get a good overall stretch, even if you are just walking in your garden or round the block. You can also integrate standing postures and lifts into your walk, to your baby's delight.

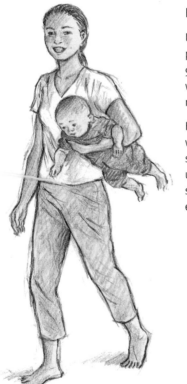

Relaxed walking

Use any of the relaxed holding positions shown on pages 90–91. As you gain confidence you will be able to hold your baby more freely, as shown here.

Hold your baby at waist level, with your forearm across his stomach and your hand tucked under his armpit. Relax your shoulders and jaw, and breathe evenly.

Trekking rhythm
To avoid getting tired if you are in a hurry to get somewhere with your baby, adopt the trekking rhythm that Amazonian mothers use.
Bend your knees slightly more than usual, keeping your back straight, and increase your pace by taking more small steps rather than lengthening your stride. Almost shuffle your feet on the ground as you walk, with minimal movements of your upper body.

Find a comfortable stride as you walk, with your hips level and your shoulders free of tension. Be aware of your breathing, and put a spring in your step by bending and stretching your knees alternately. This is fun for your baby and helps tone your abdominal muscles.

As your baby grows heavier, bend your knees slightly more to go up or downhill.

Skipping and running

To give your baby the experience of greater movement as you walk, skip for a few moments while you are carrying him. Babies love the contrast between stillness, when they are held relaxed and watch all that is happening around them, and very active moments.

Skipping stretches your legs in a pleasant rhythm for you and your baby together. If you enjoy running, take your baby for a gentle jog, using an adequate sling.

Caution: don't skip or run with your baby in a rucksack carrier until his head completely clears the top edge, as the movement will toss him about too much. A soft carrier, whether at the front or back, is ideal for running with your baby.

Dancing

Dancing is an age-old way of both stimulating and pacifying babies as well as enjoying yourself with your baby. Try different music and discover your baby's favorites. Older babies love dancing with you in front of a mirror in which they can see themselves moving.

Funny walks

All babies have a sense of humor, and 'funny walks' – purposely different movements with an element of fun – with him in your arms are a sure way to bring it out in your baby and make him more aware of his body and his reactions. Long before your baby invents his own clowning postures as a toddler, he can relate to funny ways of walking in the same way as he relates to dancing as a distinct activity.

Yoga is not all serious, and many classic postures are deliberate imitations of animal movements, some of them very expressive. For inspiration, watch any TV cartoon program with animal characters. The key to funny walks is to relax as you move. Then, using a syncopated rhythm, walking backward, and alternating fast and slow paces in rapid succession are all guaranteed ways to amuse your baby.

Energizing walks

You can walk with your baby with adapted yoga postures to build
up or expand your energy. Movement and rhythm make it possible
for you to 'walk' your baby and do postures that you would not be
able to hold without tension while carrying him and not moving.
These walking poses benefit your baby too: he will experience not
only the outline of the pose and its dynamics but also its energy.
Since each yoga posture has its own unique flow of energy, you are
enriching considerably your baby's body memory for life with these
walking poses.

1 Knee-raising walk

Breathing deeply in your lower
abdomen in this pose will tone
your lower back as well as your
abdominal muscles.

As you walk with your baby,
bend your knees up. Now and
again take a small break in
which you rest your foot on a
chair or step. Inhale and as you
exhale lift your baby up.

Repeat two or three times, walk
around again and change legs,
using the same support.

2 Cross-crawl

This strenuous walk introduces
a spinal twist.

Raise the knees as before, and
swing your baby to the side of
the bent knee, which you turn
inward. As you walk, extend
your back leg. Inhale as you
raise each knee, exhale as
you change legs.

Warrior walk

You will find that once these movements are familiar, they will soothe a fractious baby in seconds.

First, walk with your legs alternately raised to create a seat for your baby. As you walk, swing your baby from knee to knee.

Now raise your baby into the air in front of you, stretching forward from the hips.

Keep walking forward, and raise your baby above your head, lifting your abdominal and pelvic floor muscles.

Walking relaxation

A short walking relaxation (see page 66) is an ideal way to conclude walking sequences with your baby, giving the sense of completion essential to yoga practice. The more dynamic and energetic you are with your baby, the more necessary relaxation is, for offerng a balance of activity and rest.

Swings galore

As the weeks go by, your baby's enjoyment of swings may replace the pleasure he used to get from rocking. While rocking may remain the best way to soothe him when he is tired or upset, or just in a cuddly mood, swings with you are what he will increasingly crave, even before he is ready to go in a baby swing by himself. The following adapted yoga poses will swing your baby to the best advantage of both your backs. You can combine them with lifts and throws as a culmination of sequences that you create with your baby at the end of this phase of growth. When your baby is almost able to sit, swings can help him acquire the final strength and balance he needs. They also give your baby safe thrills, and anticipate the stimulation he will seek later on in the playground.

Caution: always hold your baby on each side of the rib cage under the arms, rather than from the arms. This protects his shoulder ligaments, encourages the optimal alignment of the spine and promotes solid contact between parent and baby.

Held swings

Holding your baby firmly under the arms facing away from you, stand with your legs wide apart. Bend over and swing him forward and back, gently at first and then more energetically, bending your knees with the movement to protect your back.

If your baby enjoys this swing and also likes lifts, continue the forward movement into a lift, letting your baby drop down to swing back and forth again.

You can then alternate swings and lifts with a surprise effect. Babies over five months enjoy such games very much.

Sit-swings

With your baby lying on his back, stand behind him with your feet wide apart. Bend your knees and pick him up, supporting him with your forearms under his arms. Raise your baby to a sitting position. Bring his feet together with your hands, opening his knees in a butterfly pose and continuing to support him under the arms.

Swing him back and forth between your legs, gently at first. When this is well received, swing him from side to side or in a circle in both directions, in front of your legs. With practice, you can raise and lower your baby as he swings in a circle.

Yoga together

If you have developed your practice of baby yoga simultaneously with a friend, your spouse or your partner, you may enjoy doing poses in pairs. It is even more fun to get together regularly with other people to do yoga with them as well as with their babies.

The poses shown here are only suggestions of what you can do when you have developed your own practice of yoga with your baby. The possibilities are infinite, and part of the enjoyment of yoga is to discover new ways of doing it together, in a mutually supportive environment.

Doing yoga together aids non-verbal communication, with other adults as well as with babies. Whereas a postnatal 'coffee morning' can involve a lot of sitting for babies, a group yoga session is 'play' in which parents are fully involved. Yoga together invariably involves laughter for the adults, which babies love.

Involving your baby in your yoga

If you want to do yoga yourself as well as with your baby, you can involve your baby in your own poses. The communication you have with your baby when you involve him in 'your' yoga practice can create a foundation for other activities that you do for yourself and yet from which your baby does not feel excluded. Although you are not devoting all your attention to your baby – indeed, you are doing something for yourself – you are not ignoring him either. This allows a progressive understanding of the different ways you can interact with each other. Through your yoga, your baby will discover that he is free to make choices, to ignore you and play by himself, copy you or claim your attention. In time, the more secure he becomes with this freedom, the more he will enjoy being involved in your practice.

Freedom and space

Your baby may want to be close to you for some or all of your poses, or for none of them. You may always want to do yoga with him when he is awake, or only sometimes, or decide that it is best for you to do your yoga when he is asleep or cared for by someone else. Give both your baby and yourself the chance to change minds too. Continue to hold your baby as little as safety requires if he is close to you in your poses. It is important to give him both physical and mental space while he is involved with you so that you do not encourage passive dependency. Cuddle him if he wants comforting, but otherwise give him space.

Communication through yoga

While you do yoga you are communicating your intent to your baby, even if you are not fully aware of it. If yoga has been an important part of your life before he was born, involving him in your practice is part of integrating past and present. You may choose to have an affirmation, which you can change at regular intervals, at the start of your yoga practice involving your baby, for example: 'Today I make space for you in my world, and welcome this change.'

Caution: always keep an eye on what your baby is doing, and be careful when you come down from inverted poses, particularly if your baby is mobile.

Watchpoints

• Have a fairly short set routine for two weeks at a time, so that your baby can recognize the poses after a few days.

• Select poses in which you find it easy to get him involved.

• Don't show impatience if your baby interrupts you in the middle of a pose; comforting your baby is always a priority and shows him that his needs are met. You cannot 'spoil' a baby. If you become frustrated because this happens repeatedly and you feel that your baby does not let you do your yoga when he is with you, read chapter 5 carefully and practice relaxation with your baby. Joint relaxation is likely to produce a happier interaction between you both at other times.

• Give your baby clear signals that you are beginning and ending your practice, for example by unrolling and later rolling up a mat or rug.

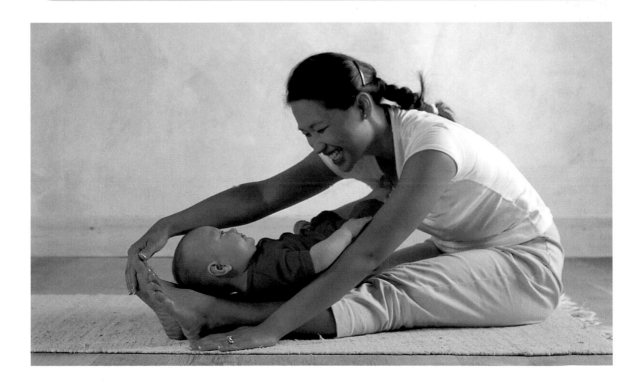

Toward independent yoga

By welcoming the participation of your baby in your own yoga, you are encouraging his progressive moves toward independent yoga. Your baby has shown signs of autonomous movement from the very beginning, when he first kicked during the hip sequence as a newborn after being stimulated by the movements you did with him. He has graduated to rolling, sitting and crawling. You have accompanied each of his steps, and perhaps anticipated them, with yoga. For some time now he will have been strengthening his back and legs finally to stand up and start walking. It may seem that this must be the end of baby yoga, as your baby becomes a toddler, but it is still possible to continue doing yoga with him.

The basic routine

Some toddlers love a combination of massage and yoga while others get up and go. Be open to your baby's own wishes.
- Give your baby opportunities to carry more of his own weight, with:
    handstands and wheelbarrows
    standing postures standing balances
    the upside-down sequence

standing self-lifts
- Invite your baby to copy you, with:
'Wind the bobbin up'
your yoga poses, such as Dog pose (below)
- Highlight the contrast between stretching and relaxing, by:
    stretching to the sky/relaxing in a woolly ball
    kick flop

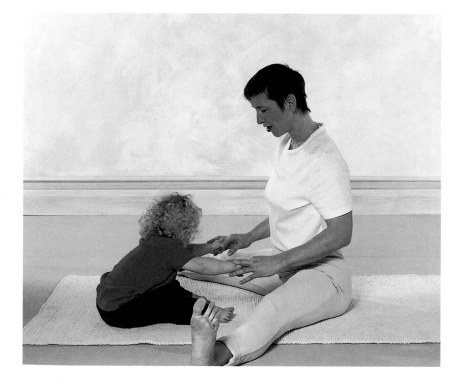

'Aimee became supple with baby yoga. She enjoys getting into yoga positions and copies my poses, which makes it tremendous fun for both of us. Yoga also taught me how to lift and carry her in a safe and comfortable manner, while stretching and strengthening all the relevant muscles.'

Unwinding and relaxing

As yoga with your baby becomes increasingly energetic and dynamic, it becomes more of a challenge to end each session with relaxation. Your growing baby is becoming more active altogether, and you may find that he is beginning to resist your attempts to have him sleep during the day as he did earlier, particularly if he has now settled to an all-night sleep. Since you can easily overstimulate a baby aged between four and eight months, it is important to limit the number of times you do exciting movements such as lifts and drops, throws and swings. If your baby has too many of these, he'll reach a point when he gets into a frenzy of activity that will end in frustration and inevitably in crying. Take care to keep a balance between activity and rest in yoga, and always allow your baby time to 'unwind' in relaxation at the end of each session.

We know that yoga postures have a calming effect on the nervous system. In yoga with babies, however, the postures are adapted with movement and the element of stillness in the held poses of classic yoga is lost. The parent must provide this stillness with 'relaxed holding' and, as the next chapter describes, with relaxation. At the end of a session, the simple technique of 'holding relaxed with intent' can help your baby unwind, either before your joint relaxation or instead of it, if your session is cut short for any reason.

Lying down in Shavasana, the Corpse pose, is always the best way to complete your yoga practice with an older baby or toddler. There are always many reasons to cut it short and get on with your day's activities, but the more you relax the more you will both benefit.

Holding relaxed with intent

Using any of the positions for relaxed holding (pages 90–1), stand or walk slowly in a circle, holding your baby as comfortably and loosely as you can against your body. The difference is that you are now learning to use your intent. This means communicating silently to your baby, with your mind and body, that it is time to unwind and relax after activity. Use the techniques introduced earlier to center yourself, using your breathing to release tension in your body (pages 16–17 and page 67) as you either stand, sit or walk slowly. Feel the rhythm of your breathing and lengthen your exhalation slightly to slow down

your breathing even more. If your baby protests and gesticulates, or cries and even screams, hold him gently but firmly and continue to do what you have chosen to do, whether standing, sitting or walking with him, remaining steady and centered. You can also talk calmly to your baby as you hold him and explain that now it is time to rest. The more you practice joint relaxation with him as described in chapter 5, the more effective your intent becomes as you hold your baby 'relaxed'.

Trouble with unwinding

It can be stressful to watch your baby getting into a frantic state that you cannot make sense of or bring to an end. If nothing you have done to help is working and you feel tension mounting up in your body, try singing – any tune that comes to mind will do – and allow yourself to move in a rhythm that is soothing for you while holding your baby. The rhythm may be a lively or gentle one; what matters is that you are able to hold your baby steady and relax minute by minute in this rhythm.

When you have got rid of your own tension, you can sit down with your baby, continuing to use rhythmical movements with him such as balances, as shown above. Now it is your baby's turn to calm down: in the rhythmical action of your arms you will gradually sense tranquillity returning until you feel him relaxing. In this way, yoga soothes your baby's whole nervous system (much more effectively than a dummy or pacifier, which merely suppresses discomfort and agitation). Every time you repeat this unwinding process, releasing your tension and then your baby's, it will become easier.

5 Surrender and self-nurture
More about relaxation

The thought of a baby practicing yogic relaxation may sound strange at first, but it is the perfect counterpart to the more active yoga postures. If you integrate relaxation into your yoga practice with your baby, it becomes an essential component that makes it complete. The point is to relax jointly with your baby: your own relaxation is just as important as hers is.

Every yoga posture combines and contrasts stretching and relaxing. Moreover, each sequence ends with a rest and each session with a longer relaxation, usually in the Corpse pose. Relaxation enlivens the subtle energies of the body, and can become a powerful tool for enriching your parenting in a great variety of ways. It is also a skill that your baby acquires for life, at a time when her central nervous system is at its most receptive. The earlier you start relaxing with your baby after birth, the easier it is to experience the benefits of relaxation and the more profound these benefits can be. If you are starting when your baby is over six months old, follow the basic steps described on pages 106–7 first, before reading this chapter.

At the end of her daily yoga routine, particularly if you do some massage as well as the exercises and bathe her too, your baby is likely to be pleasantly tired and to fall asleep after a satisfying feed. This is good for her, but relaxation as an acquired skill can achieve even more. Just as with an adult, deep relaxation will alter your baby's body functions in a similar way to sleep, but within a waking state of consciousness. Her heartbeat will slow down and her breathing will become more even, she will get very warm and her flow of energy will change. You will also notice that her overall behavior becomes calmer and more contented.

Although you may have chosen to develop your baby's practice of yoga rather than your own with this book, in deep relaxation you cannot separate your baby's practice from yours. The two work together, reinforce each other and have an effect on you both, together and individually. Relaxation with your baby is quintessentially an interactive practice: it originates within the exchange between your body and your baby's body and transforms it in the process.

The process of relaxation

If you have never experienced deep relaxation, you may need to make a leap of faith while you follow the basic steps until you feel the physical process of relaxing in your own body. You will realize that it involves your whole self, including your emotions and your mind, in a way that differs profoundly from just resting or having a quiet cuddle with your baby. If you already practice yogic relaxation regularly, you can apply the techniques you know to relaxing with your baby as described here.

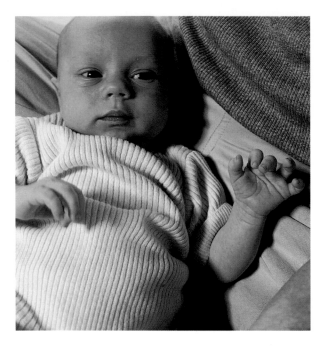

Relaxing with your baby is different from relaxing on your own, because you are focusing on the interaction between you. Disengaging from the world, from activity, also means to let go of 'minding' her. The challenge is to take your attention away from her when you are holding her close to you and you are both awake. If you think of yourself as a car, it is like putting yourself in neutral gear, letting your engine idle. This does not mean that you are withdrawing your 'self' from your baby, but that your baby will be able to disengage from sharing your pattern of energy, which she has learned since she was in the womb. She will experience you free of superficial worry, and enjoy the deep nurturing silence and peace lying under the currents of stress that sustain your activity from day to day. At this time of mutual adjustment between you, particularly if she is your first child, relaxation with your baby is a priority for your well–being, hers and that of your whole family.

What happens between you and your baby

Be aware of all the possibilities of relaxation:

- *You relax, so your baby relaxes.* This is often the reason why parents do relaxation with their baby in the first place, but it takes considerable experience and skill before a distressed baby can be calmed instantly. This is your ultimate goal.

- *You start relaxing, you feel your baby relax, this makes you more relaxed, your baby responds by relaxing more, and so on...* An exchange takes place between you and your baby that helps you both, deepening the process of relaxation as a mutual experience.

You can start observing, experimenting and experiencing 'being relaxed' together with your baby through your day. If you notice when it happens and when it doesn't, and when you don't know how to make it happen, you'll discover the best situations for allowing relaxation to take place.

Using self-referral

Babies define their perception of the world in response to what they experience. Remember the principle of 'self-referral' mentioned at the beginning of this book (page 19). The more you become aware of your own state of being, the more you will realize that your baby responds directly to it. She is aware of your inner disposition. This can be a revelation to you and change your attitude to your baby, as you no longer look at her behavior separately but at the interaction between you, a two-way process.

You are as 'good' a parent as you can be in your circumstances, and it is futile to try to relax all the time with your baby. In any case, babies need a balance of stress and relaxation in a rhythm that resembles that of day and night, waking and sleeping. So watch and register how you feel when your baby frustrates you, but at the same time live fully and own your emotions. There is no place for guilt or blame in the present, only potential for change.

- *Your baby is relaxed, so you relax.* Becoming humble about the interaction with your baby also enables you to learn from her how to relax more. This is explained in detail on page 120.

- *You and your baby relax together, so other members of your family relax.* The effects of your joint relaxation with your baby soon extend to other members of your household.

- *Now when you relax, you are able truly to relax your baby.* This is expecially useful if she is upset or unwell.

Learning to use relaxation as a spiritual tool in this way can help you develop other dimensions of yoga, and expand your consciousness even more.

'For me, an important aspect of baby yoga has been the relaxation. I have truly learned to relax and I feel that I can switch off from Maria, knowing that she is happy and safe near me. I am amazed at how she has learned to respect my space when I'm relaxing, and find that she relaxes too.'

Getting ready to relax together

Besides the short relaxations that complete each yoga sequence, 'joint relaxation' can be a sequence in its own right. You can practice it with your baby at any time, either with the exercises or separately. It will take about ten minutes to go through the basic steps. Once you are familiar with them, you will be able to reach your 'relaxation space' quickly, and spend more time in deep relaxation.

1 Rapid self-awareness

As you prepare to start relaxing, rapidly experience how you are feeling right now, first in relation to your baby and then to yourself. At first, you may feel confused, especially if you are short of sleep and you are finding parenthood very challenging. Acknowledge that you can't feel anything except exhaustion if this is the case. Later nuances of mood and energy levels will become more easily perceptible. It can be difficult for new mothers to distinguish how they feel in themselves from how they feel in relation to their babies. Acknowledge this too. If you have found the Mountain pose helpful to center and ground yourself, use it to complete your 'rapid self-awareness' before getting into a relaxing position.

2 Positions for joint relaxation

After gaining experience, you will be able to relax with your baby in any position. At first, however, make yourself as comfortable as possible together.

Lying down

Even if you are experienced in yogic relaxation, lying flat on your back may not be the most comfortable position to relax in with a young baby. With your lower back well supported, bend your knees if needed, and have your neck and head in line with your spine,

Before you begin
Remove all obstacles to relaxation, such as safety concerns, by for example placing cushions on each side of you, switching on the answerphone, and checking that you will not be disturbed. After a few times, your mental checklist will become automatic and you will cease to invent obstacles because the rewards of relaxation will motivate you to eliminate them outright.

neither dropped backward nor with your chin tucked in tight. Another good relaxing position with a baby is lying against a beanbag or a large pillow, so that the base of your spine is close to the floor and your body at a 20- to 30-degree angle.

Rest your baby on your chest, either face up or face down as you both prefer it. Very young babies often enjoy lying on their back or side. Be prepared to change positions as your baby grows, both for her sake and yours. Alternatively, have your baby next to you rather than on your body. Some form of body contact with her, however, helps join the two of you in relaxation.

Sitting

Sitting to relax during or after feeding your baby is comfortable if your lower back is well supported and your knees are level with your hips. Make sure you have something to rest your feet on in order to raise your knees if needed. If you sit on a low chair, you can also extend your legs over a cushion or beanbag. If you have had a cesarean section, place your baby on a cushion on your lap to help relieve pressure on your lower abdomen.

Standing and walking

Walking relaxation (see page 66), a way of relaxing with your baby using movement and rhythm, can also include all the steps described here for still relaxation.

3 Signalling relaxation to your baby

Your baby may quickly recognize when you are getting into your joint relaxing position, particularly if you give her definite signals in a set order, such as the following:

1 Free your back and neck by adjusting your chosen position. Drop your lower jaw and yawn if needed.

2 Exhale deeply two or three times, letting your lungs take the air in rather than breathing in forcefully in between. Voice your exhalations if you wish, perhaps with a yawn or sigh.

3 Loosen your hold on your baby. She should be resting in such a way that you do not need to hold her (except in walking relaxation). Do so in a loving way, perhaps stroking her body or head, or rocking her gently from side to side.

4 Feel the rhythm of your breath and register your baby's if you can. If you know how, you might want to chant at this point, or hum a note that feels good to you.

5 If you like, visualize an image that evokes security, closeness and happiness for you in relation to your baby. Set your intent on opening a space to enjoy relaxing together, freely and harmoniously.

Picking up your baby's cues
As you follow these steps, observe any pattern of behavior that your baby tends to repeat, such as:
- fidgeting before settling comfortably
- crying for food or attention
- opening her arms wide
- cooing or singing
- a slower heartbeat and warmer skin

Opening the space of joint relaxation

Once you are settled and ready to relax with your baby, there is a threshold through which you have to go before you can enter deep relaxation. Sharing the space of relaxation with your baby can be challenging, and you need to take particular care to get it right from the beginning. Experience is what matters. Use this page as a practical guide when you start, and read the following pages to enrich your experience afterward, and again as your baby grows older and your practice develops.

Identity

The arrival of your baby changes all your existing relationships. It may be that you are so much in love with your baby that you cannot detach from her at all, or you may doubt that life will ever return to 'normal'. Many parents experience these feelings, which at times may threaten their sense of identity. As you start relaxing and 'centering' yourself, you will become quietly aware of both the closeness and the separateness of your identity and your baby's.

Steps to letting go

1 Identity
This is you, my baby, and this is me
I experience fully our closeness and our separateness

2 Trust
You are all right, I am all right
I experience fully our readiness just to be, without any wanting or doing for a while

3 Daring to let go
I can safely let go of minding you
I experience fully the difference between minding and caring from a deeper awareness

4 Releasing stress
Where does your crying go in my body?
I experience fully the tension that accumulates daily in looking after you, and it can be released

5 Surrender
I release tension and feel relaxed
I experience fully the process of surrendering to what is

6 Self-nurture
I experience fully the infinite abundance of the universal life force around us
I draw from it to nurture myself and the bond between us

7 Unconditional love
I experience fully how we are one
Loving you unconditionally gives me great joy

Steps to centering yourself in relation to your baby

- Press your feet on the floor, bending your knees. Hold your baby's hand or hands, being aware of your two bodies.

- Acknowledge any negative emotions you may have; for each one, find a positive counterpart.

- Close your eyes, feel how you are with your baby. Open your eyes, look at the two of you as you are now. Close your eyes again and experience your perception and your feeling together. As a mother, recall the feeling of your baby inside you and contrast it with your feeling and perception of your baby now outside you.

- Focus on your first and second chakras, in your perineum and navel, and breathe deeply into them, feeling the roots of yourself.

Trust

Yoga with your baby celebrates safe risk and promotes trust and self-confidence, which extend to other areas of your life together. If you find yourself worrying about your new responsibilities, you need to focus on trust in yourself, in your baby and in getting the support you need for relaxing with your baby. Trust is not only about having confidence that you are doing your best for your baby, your family and yourself, but also about being confident that you are perfectly taken care of in the cosmic orchestration of the universe. If you cannot quite believe this, you could call it a positive attitude to life.

'I find joint relaxation especially useful for my baby, who is otherwise constantly on the go. It trains him not to need entertaining all the time, and I love to be able to sit with him calmly, feeling content and at peace. People also remark on how easy going he is.'

Daring to let go

Now you are beginning to enter the 'space of relaxation'. If during this process of letting go your baby starts crying, stop and comfort her. Try again later when she is happy. She will soon learn your behavior, and after experiencing it as a shared, pleasurable activity will welcome the steps that lead to it. If your baby persistently begins to cry when you start relaxing with her, she may need to heal a traumatic experience of which you may or may not be aware. See page 120 for suggestions on how to help her welcome joint relaxation.

Letting go of your baby is hard to begin with, because it defies your normal state of consciousness. You want reassurance that you can do it without any harmful effects, and you may not be sure that it's possible unless you fall asleep. You won't know unless you try, and it may take a few trials before you feel it happening. Then you will need to explore it over time.

Releasing stress

• Close your eyes. Relax your eyes in their sockets, feeling your eyelids. Follow your optic nerves deep inside your brain. Rest the back of your head more on the beanbag or pillow and relax your neck once more. With your eyes closed, feel your baby, whether you are holding her or not. After some time your perception of your baby with your eyes closed becomes keener and richer. According to yoga, you learn to see with your 'inner eye'.

• Dissociate the aspect of your hearing that makes you attentive to sounds around you from hearing as a conscious activity. Like a dog asleep yet attentive to noises around the house, you remain faintly aware of external sounds while drawing your hearing inward. It is now part of your intuition, or inner knowing.

• Become aware of your breathing, just as it is. Do not try and change it in any way or judge it. Enjoy feeling the rhythm of your breath, close to your baby. When you feel your breath, you become, so to speak, your own witness. You step out of

activity and watch yourself 'being' without involving your mind. At first, thoughts and emotions can interfere with your experience, but if you allow yourself to follow your breathing quietly, particularly when your baby is peaceful or asleep with you, it becomes easier and easier. You may find that it calms you in no time at all, even if you felt at your wits' end just a moment ago.

• Now you can start going deeper into the relaxation. You have done it, you have 'let go' of minding. You did not lose contact with your baby in the process. On the contrary, by withdrawing your senses inward and quietly focusing on your breathing, you find yourself closer to your baby, without the barrier of your constant stream of thoughts between you and her.

At this point, the relaxation becomes yours and hers jointly. You can now include her in your awareness of yourself breathing. Feel her breathing too. It is likely that your breathing rhythms have 'entrained', synchronizing with each other, from the time of birth.

Surrender

It now becomes possible to 'surrender' to what is. In the same way that you witnessed your breath just as it was, you can experience yourself being relaxed, together with your baby, now. This may be easy to do if you are tired, and it is fine if you both fall asleep. In fact, this is one of the ways in which you can get back to sleep after being woken in the night. But if you are very tired or affected by strong emotion, surrendering becomes the most challenging step. Do not worry if this is your experience. Acknowledge that you cannot believe that you are blessed with your life as it is, but the same time, welcome the possibility of receiving help and solutions. Surrender to the hope, if not the faith, that you can receive all the help you need.

In the 'space' of relaxation, surrendering in this way makes you more receptive to the dynamic web of love and goodwill that surrounds you and your baby. Even for a short time, accessing this space makes you contact that part of yourself that responds to deep rest and knows that under all other emotions and even through pain, a sweet harmony can be found again. If as you relax you become aware of deep-seated anger, which may be specifically at someone or non-specific, surrendering can also be helpful. Acknowledging your emotion without judging yourself will lead you to appropriate forms of resolution.

Self-nurture

Surrendering opens the floodgates of the universal life force (prana), which you can then fully receive and put to use for yourself and your baby straight away. Again, all you have to do is 'feel'. This feeling is like 'plugging in' or putting a battery on a charger. You can only know it by experiencing it and enjoying the benefits of it for yourself. Instantly, you feel more rested than you have been since before your baby was born. You might also feel some tingling in your hands and your facial muscles relaxing further. Mainly, you feel nurtured physically, emotionally and spiritually in a way that addresses your most immediate needs.

Gorge yourself with this self-nurturing each time you relax, and learn to generate the nurturing you need in order to nurture your child. As yoga adepts of the classic Indian tradition say, 'learn to become your own mother and your own father'. In the same way that you need to release tension, ideally each day, you also need to replace the nurturing you give your baby, storing more for the demands ahead.

Extending self-nurture to others

You can extend this self-nurture to your baby through you. For a mother, this is like nourishing your baby through an invisible umbilical cord. A father may experience it in this way too, or as an

---

Relaxation and postnatal depression

If you experience postnatal depression, doing joint relaxation as a yoga sequence will help you gain the deep rest you need, while still being actively involved with your baby.

• Action rhymes counting and registering your baby's toes or fingers, such as 'This little piggy', or 'One, two, three, four, five, once I caught a fish alive' can help you engage more physically with your baby after settling down to relax, using both touch and sound.

• Register at least two reasons for feeling good today in your immediate surroundings. The second one may not be as easy to find as the first, but with perseverance you can always spot it.

• Put a drop of an uplifting aromatherapy oil on a tissue and place it under your nose after you are settled for relaxation with your baby. Clary sage, frankincense and most of all rose are especially soothing.

• Be aware of your third chakra, in the solar plexus region. Breathe deeply into this area, which is associated with trust and self-belief.

• Try to make use of the unconditional love for your baby that is released in relaxation to nurture your own 'inner baby', which may still be in need of such love. Quietly direct unconditional love to yourself as part of your own nurturing as a new mother.

energy field that he shares with his baby. If you are familiar with visualization, use any image that comes to you at this stage for this purpose. As you do this, your baby is likely to become visibly affected. If she is awake, she may go very quiet, lying or playing peacefully. If she is asleep, she may go into a deeper level of sleep and feel warmer and floppier.

Once you are familiar with self-nurturing, you can extend it to other people close to you, such as your spouse or partner, other children, your own parents or close friends. Redirecting some of this good feeling to them, sharing it with them, is possible in relaxation without depleting you as it may do in activity. Until you are experienced, the time to do this is when the image of someone close to you presents itself as you are relaxing.

Unconditional love

The more you become able to nurture yourself and your baby in joint relaxation, the more you are able to experience the unconditional love that bonds her to you and you to her in a real, physical way. Relaxation helps you access the deeper levels of feeling that underlie the fluctuations of day-to-day emotions and physical states. As you access deep rest, it is easier to remember that you love your baby and truly feel this love. Beyond exasperation and exhaustion, and even through postnatal depression, you will find this undercurrent of love through relaxation and be able to find it again and again. It is a fount to which you can always return as your child grows older.

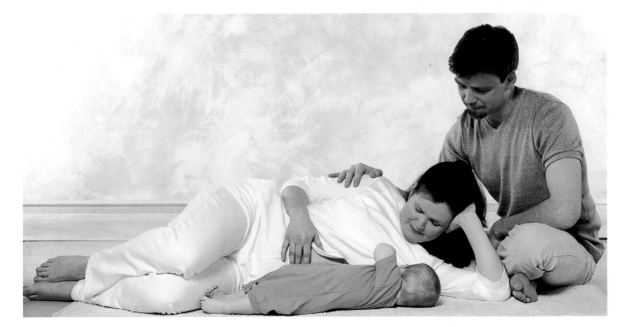

Exchanging relaxation with your baby

The relaxation already described was focused on you and invited you to include your baby in a process that you unfolded. You can also learn to relax 'from' your baby and actively develop ways of exchanging relaxation with her, so that after she gives you the impetus to relax, you allow yourself to relax fully and then, through physical contact, you help her relax more in turn.

Experience your baby's relaxed body
When your baby falls asleep in your arms, you can feel the difference between her superficial sleep and her deep sleep. You may have felt your baby relax completely while awake, for example while feeding, floating in water, or after a massage or her yoga practice. Whenever this happens, register it carefully and experience it as fully as you can, paying attention to all the cues your baby gives you about becoming relaxed.

Learn from your baby...
Besides observing your baby, practice deliberately imitating and reproducing the signals she is giving you. Wherever you find yourself with your feeding or sleepy baby, make yourself more comfortable and allow your body to become soft and floppy.

Contrast these bodily changes with those you observe when your baby experiences discomfort and register how they affect you. As you hold your distressed baby in your arms, feel how much it affects you physically, and your responses as you try to counteract her distress. Make a note of where and how much you tense up, according to how much you are affected. Write them down in order to get a more precise image.

...what your baby learns from you
Your baby has been watching you intently since birth and has learnt the signals you give her about being relaxed or tense. In fact it soon becomes impossible to separate your baby's responses to you from yours to her, although for some time you may still have the illusion that she is this way or that way irrespective of you. Your baby has tendencies and a character of her own, but the way in which these develop has much to do with her interaction with her main carers. In the same way as in yoga postures, the more you stretch, the

more you can relax, and the more you can contrast clearly tension and relaxation in your interaction with your baby, the more you can learn to exchange relaxation with her.

Two-way relaxation

Practice responding to your baby by physically relaxing when you feel her relaxing, for example during feeding or with yoga. When she is happy and smiles, you will be drawn to smile back. Look at her body language and go through similar motions, loosening your back, opening your hands and perhaps shaking them, yawning, frowning and releasing your frown, and relaxing your neck. Continue with your own ways of relaxing, making yourself as comfortable as you can in your interaction with her. Watch her responses to what you do.

After repeating this exchange a few times, make it more theatrical, exaggerating your imitation of her and your own ways of relaxing, so that it becomes a game. (You can also play this game in a more active way during your baby's favorite yoga sequences, imitating and playing back to her your own version of her delight.)

Lullabies

Using a 'signature song' may help you go through the motions you have selected, either using a song you know or making your own. This is the way in which people all over the world use lullabies. Rediscovering this ancient art is a marvellous way of exchanging relaxation with your baby, as lullabies exert their charm on you as much as they relax your baby.

Calming your baby

You can use the same behavior to pacify your baby or jolly her along when she is unhappy. As you hold your distressed baby, play back to her all the cues for relaxation that you picked up through interacting with her when she was relaxed. Because you have made them your own she is likely to be sensitive to them and respond to them. Babies are sophisticated imitators, and just going through the motions will have some effect, because

• It short-circuits your usual reaction to her distress, particularly if it has become a pattern.

• You are presenting her with a behavior that she will recognize, since it comes from both herself and you.

• It is a good way to disinguish genuine discomfort from boredom or a need for closeness.

After you gain experience, you can integrate this exchange into any 'relaxed holding' position you choose, going through the motions of relaxing yourself, inspired by your baby and in a more inward way.

Instant relaxation with your baby

Practice will make it possible for you to make use of relaxation instantly, wherever and whenever you need it. This is as true for going into a deep yogic relaxation with your baby as for exchanging relaxation with her by means of behavior inspired by her. Don't be discouraged, however, if you are not immediately successful. It may not always work, but each time you succeed in defusing tension between yourself and your baby and restore peace and contentment, you consolidate the process and make relaxation a more powerful tool for both of you.

Use one or a combination of these basic steps to instant relaxation, or find your own.

In any position
1 Exhale deeply two or three times, breathing abdominally
2 Relax your holding
3 Feel your heart center
4 'Plug in' the infinite source of unconditional love so that your body becomes a 'transmitter' to your baby through your contact with her

If sitting or standing
1 Drop your shoulders
2 Bend your knees while keeping your back straight
3 Let your whole back drop two or three times on an out-breath

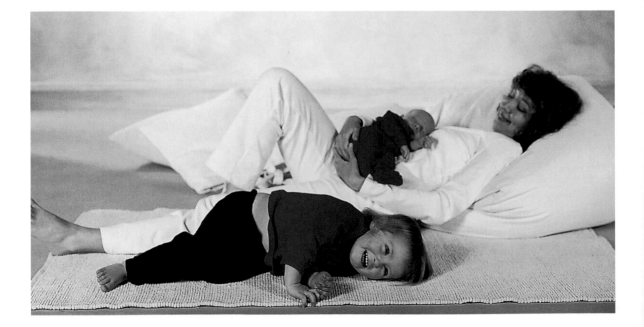

Creating a 'relaxed field'

If you wish to pursue an activity at home that does not involve your baby, and you would rather not use a playpen or a chair, you may find this practice helpful.

Both the yoga postures and the practice of joint relaxation have made you aware that your interaction with your baby affects her contentment and well–being. You can use this awareness to create a 'relaxed field' that extends around your baby while you are in the same room or space. This can also be a useful way of resting with a very active baby, or when your baby needs special closeness, for example when she is unwell.

Besides these times of need, creating a 'relaxed field' around your baby greatly contributes to the expanding spiral of joy with her in day-to-day living. Although you may be sceptical at first, after two or three weeks of practicing it you will notice a new calmness and contentment in your baby, and so will family and friends.

• With your baby not in direct contact with you but in the same room, sit down comfortably and follow the steps for deep relaxation described in this chapter. Choose a moment when you are alone with your baby and when she is not crying.

• Make sure she is safe, particularly if she can roll over or crawl. If you are anxious about this, ask someone else to watch your baby from a distance, without interacting with her, for example in the next room, leaving the doors open.

• As you enter relaxation, register your resistance to let go of 'minding' and to closing your eyes, letting your baby be unattended. Trust that you are switching to a different, complementary way of caring for her and allow yourself to relax deeply, closing your eyes.

• As you find the deeper current of bonding with your baby in the space of relaxation, let go of it. This may be hard to do at first. Persevere until you experience a 'field', like a magnetic field, which surrounds you and your baby. If it helps, visualize a bubble or circle to make this field more real for you.

• Rather than focusing on the 'invisible cord' as you did earlier, both you and your baby are now together in a 'relaxed field'. The more deeply you relax, the greater the effect will be on your baby. She will be likely to find contentment with her own company, and with whatever she is doing at the time, while you will wonder at how free yet close you feel in relation to her.

• The older your baby is when you start practicing this relaxation, the more she will resist it. She may clamor for your superficial attention as she is used to. If she becomes distressed, pick her up and reassure her that you love her. At the same time, be aware of your own resistance to 'let her be'. The peace that comes with each of you being self-contained in the 'relaxed field' can be very liberating for both of you.

• As the mother of a growing baby or toddler, the chores of everyday life as much as relaxation become opportunities to create 'relaxed fields' between you both. Soon you will find that a silent dialogue flows through the day, creating a deeper harmony.

6 Dealing with problems
Yoga for health and joy

While yoga won't prevent or cure all problems, it can make a great difference for the better. Yoga gives you a practical means of restoring the physical and spiritual harmony between you and your baby, which may be compromised if the delicate balance of your lives together has been disrupted.

Much expert advice on baby care and parenting revolves around problems. Babies are often labelled sleepless, fussy or colicky, and it's usually suggested that you must put up with such problems if no solution to them can be found. The approach taken in this book is radically different. Following the Ayurvedic principles underlying the practice of yoga, we can see the baby's life holistically rather than focusing on dysfunction. Priority is given to prevention and early detection of signs and symptoms before a situation becomes critical. The Ayurvedic approach is to concentrate mainly on nurturing and bringing about optimal conditions, in which both parents and babies can restore their respective and shared health and joy. If a crisis does arise, however, specific interventions can often relieve symptoms.

The stimulation that yoga gives babies in our sedentary lives helps improve their digestion and promote sound sleep. It is not just the physical stimulation that is effective. The fact that it creates a playful and enjoyable interaction between you and your baby is perhaps more than half the answer in the therapeutic value of yoga. All aspects of a baby's life are connected, so when one improves others get better too, and you, the parents, also get relief. It is often difficult to remember what was wrong once all is well again, and your contented baby smiles at you once more, after a sound sleep and a satisfying feed.

When life gets tough with your baby, everyone in the family suffers, but there is no point in feeling that you may be at fault. The psychologist Donald Winnicott's concept of a 'good enough' parent lets us see that mistakes and problems are inevitable as we care for our children, and that we need not aspire for perfection. Even the most experienced parent has to learn how to care for each new baby. Yoga opens a space in which parents and babies can explore ways to expand their bodies and minds together, without prejudice and with as few preconceived ideas as possible.

Crying

Babies have different cries for hunger, pain and other physical discomforts, as well as for emotional dissatisfaction or distress. Your baby's crying is a form of communication, and the pitch, timing and frequency of cries can yield information about his state of health. As you get to know your baby you will learn to decipher his signals and respond more effectively to his pleas for help. Doing yoga with your baby will enhance your communication with him and help you remain calm while you discover what he needs.

Keep talking to your baby, even if you find his crying challenging. Voicing your emotions, negative as well as positive, is better for your baby than not expressing them, since he will perceive them anyway. The more honest you are with yourself and your baby, the better your communication with him will be.

Your baby's cries and what they mean
As you get to know the differences between different types of crying, you will also learn the particular body language associated with each type, especially hand movements. Your baby may also express more than one need at a time.

- Loud, intense cry: pain (as when your baby's foot is pricked to take blood)

- Impatient cry: hunger (as when your baby wakes up from a long sleep)

- Crying with movements of whole body: tiredness and overstimulation

- Changeable cry, stopping and starting: boredom, non-specific need

- High-pitched, loud cry, becoming very high-pitched with a faster rhythm; expressive hand movements with opening and clenching; can develop into a rage; baby has tears: distress

- Alternately high- and low-pitched, baby runs out of breath, syncopated rhythm, fists clenched tight, kicking; eye contact not possible: rage

The more distressed your baby is, particularly when eye contact is not possible, the more important it is that you center yourself with breathing awareness (see page 17) before responding with yoga.

Responding to crying with yoga

Unless your baby is clearly hungry (the most common cause of crying), try first using yoga movements, along with your voice, in response to different cries. If this does not work within a couple of minutes, feed your baby.

- Pain: relaxed holding, cradling, gentle swings, joint relaxation, walking relaxation. For digestive troubles, go to page 130.

- Tiredness and overstimulation: cradling, holding relaxed face-down, walking relaxation, joint relaxation.

- Boredom and unspecified needs: any yoga sequence corresponding to your baby's age group first, before feeding. Standing postures are most effective: drops, swings, lifts and throws.

- Distress: relaxed holding first, particularly face-down for a baby under six months. Gentle drops and lifts are grounding and restore your baby's awareness of secure contact with you. Lifts distract him physically rather than by engaging his attention elsewhere.

- Rage: relaxed holding and walking relaxation. Hold your baby face-down away from you, engaging him in your walking rhythm. Now and again stop and cradle him, relaxing yourself. If he stops crying, try to make eye contact with him, rock him gently and talk to him to reassure him.

Persistent crying

Even a healthy baby may sometimes cry inconsolably, for no obvious reason. It is easy to forget that he needs spiritual nourishment through close contact with you, but this means that you need to feel spiritually nourished yourself, in order to support him in this way. Yoga is a positive means to get the nourishment you need from within.

The more physical security you give your baby, the more likely it is that he will resolve the source of his persistent crying. In order to enhance your baby's natural healing capacity, which is great, you need to be rested and relaxed so that you can be receptive and trusting in him, in yourself and in the process. In practice, this means:

- Each time your baby falls asleep after a spell of distressed crying that you cannot make sense of, have a rest yourself lying down, no matter how busy you are. If you have other children, read them a story or watch a film quietly.

- Practice joint relaxation every day. Include your other children, too. This creates a rhythm that in itself is reassuring, particularly if your baby cries on most days.

- Try not to withdraw communication and love; this is what he is trying to get more of. If possible, ground yourself with the Mountain pose or breathing to stay centered.

- If you feel a wave of aggression coming through you (which most parents do at times), simply acknowledge it and let it wash away with two or three exhalations, shaking your hands and feet so that it does not get picked up by your baby.

- When your baby does stop crying, reassure him that all is well by seeking eye contact and talking to him gently. If he stills sighs or sobs a little, exhale deeply with him. If your baby is falling asleep, he will still hear you if you speak to him, so wish him a good, restoring sleep and tell him that he is fine and that you love him.

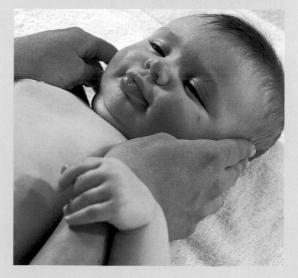

Sleep problems

You can influence your baby's sleeping pattern from birth in a number of ways so that the whole household gets enough rest. Yoga with your baby will not instantly make him sleep through the night, but can help prevent sleeping problems from arising and getting out of hand.

Every baby needs different amounts of sleep, and the range of variation in the first year is considerable. Your baby may not, however, be getting all the sleep he needs, nor may he be getting sleep of a good enough quality. Yoga offers your baby not only enough stimulating exercise to induce sound sleep each day but also physical security and comfort, so that your baby perceives going to sleep as pleasurable and welcomes rather than resists the process of falling asleep.

Mutual adjustments

You may find it difficult to go back to sleep if your baby wakes you during the night, and that you need to adjust better to your baby's sleep rhythms. There is a difference between being flexible, accepting that your baby's rhythms change as he grows, and allowing your baby to sleep just when he likes without attempting to work out a mutually satisfying routine.

In the first four months, you are establishing routines that will become important signals to your baby that it is time to go to sleep. Yoga helps your baby rely less on familiar patterns and the environment that surrounds him and more on the physical signals exchanged with you from the time you start your yoga practice. Once established, signals such as relaxed holding, releasing tension with breathing or instant relaxation will be enough to tell your baby that it is time to sleep. His body memory of the yoga is likely to be more effective than any other routine conditioning you may develop.

Even if your baby usually sleeps soundly through the night from early on, there will be times when he will wake up, for instance when he is teething. To go back to sleep more easily after being woken up, practice alternate nostril breathing (see box, above right) for two to three minutes and follow the steps for joint relaxation (page 114).

> **Alternate nostril breathing**
> This exercise acts as a natural sedative. Place your index and middle fingers on your forehead, your thumb on your right nostril and your other fingers lightly over your left nostril. Inhale deeply through your left nostril, then, pressing your left nostril and lifting your thumb from the right, exhale deeply through your right nostril. Now do the opposite, inhaling through the right nostril and exhaling through the left. Do this for six rounds, then breathe naturally.

Helping your baby sleep better

After just of few days of doing yoga with your baby, you may notice that his sleep that follows your routine is slightly longer than his usual sleep at this time.

• Combine yoga with massage and a bath in the evening to help extend your baby's sleep in the early part of the night.

• The hip sequence followed by twists and bends are also helpful at night.

• Rhythms are important in your baby's perception of the daily cycle. The more you offer him a clear contrast between activity and rest, the more he is likely to sleep with a predictable pattern.

• When patterns change because your baby is changing, particularly in the fifth month, increasing activity may help your baby settle into a new rhythm. Two vigorous yoga sequences during the day, including standing postures, walks, swings and lifts, will help give your baby the exercise he needs to get nicely tired until he starts crawling.

• To help your baby stay awake longer when you wish to alter your baby's nap pattern in a way that fits better with your family life, practice especially the energizing walks (page 96), and lifts, swings and throws in a standing position.

Making sleep pleasurable

A lively rhythm balancing sleep and waking, night and day, sustained by an adaptable routine that all members of the household can be happy with or at least tolerate, ultimately depends on how secure your baby feels about sleeping. If sleep has become an issue in your household, doing relaxation with your baby is the best way of diffusing the tension that affects your baby's perception of sleeping.

• Observe your baby as he falls asleep, registering any tension in his body through watching his hands, his breathing pattern, his eye movements and body tone. If you notice tension, you can help him relax without rousing him, by talking to him gently and perhaps rocking him slightly. You will see him unwind in his sleep.

• If your baby falls asleep easily when you are holding him, but wakes up again as soon as you put him down, doing a daily session of joint relaxation will help him feel a deeper sense of security in close contact with you. This will in turn make physical separation less threatening to him.

• If your baby resists the process of going to sleep, walking and walking relaxation can also be helpful.

Digestive problems

In the Ayurvedic medical system that underlies yoga, digestion is considered the foundation of health. It is therefore desirable to encourage a good assimilation of nutrients and elimination of waste products from the beginning of life. Feeding and digestion play a dominant part in the life of newborns, and determine to a large extent how comfortable and happy they are.

Even more than sleep, feeding is not just a physiological process but is also affected to some degree by your baby's perception of the pleasure associated with it. Besides giving your baby the satisfaction of a full stomach, feeding is the most fundamental source of spiritual nourishment for him at a time of special physical closeness with you. There are many advantages in breastfeeding your baby over giving him formula milk, for his health and yours as his mother, but even if you are bottle-feeding, the quality of physical interaction at feeding time is just as crucial. Yoga can enhance all the aspects of digestion, contributing greatly to your baby's enjoyment of life, particularly during the first six months.

Feeding watchpoints

- Sit or lie in a relaxed position.

- Release any anxiety about the supply and quality of your milk (follow one coherent source of advice and trust it). Ensure your baby gets the necessary medical checks at every stage in his development.

- The more you use feeding times to rest and bond with your baby, the more prolactin is released in your system if you breastfeed; if you bottle-feed, the endorphins produced will come to be associated with feeding.

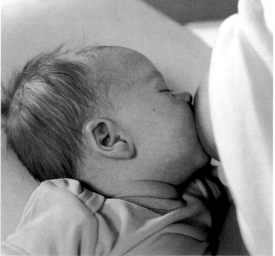

- If feeding is difficult, practice alternate nostril breathing (page 128) at the beginning of each feed to calm yourself. Instant relaxation is a good way to disengage from focusing too much on feeding, which may not help your baby regulate his intake.

- Every baby feeds differently. Take more time to relax with him if he finishes quickly and be patient with a slow feeder. Knowing your baby's feeding pattern will also help you discover how to practice the yoga sequences in a way that suits his temperament.

Regurgitating and vomiting

Some babies regurgitate partly digested milk in the half-hour after a feed, while others never do. Yoga does not seem to have any effect on whether babies regurgitate, or how much. With babies under four months, however, yoga can help bring out mucus together with the curd. If your baby has mucus and you are breastfeeding, you may wish to adjust your diet to be more mucus free, and/or use some gentle alternative therapies such as reflexology or therapies related to acupressure (such as tui na massage for babies) if you are bottle-feeding.

Caution: if your baby is vomiting, which is likely to be accompanied by diarrhea, interrupt your yoga routine and seek medical advice.

Winding or burping

The amount of air that babies swallow during feeds varies for each baby, but if you are relaxed and feeding in the correct position, your baby should need little or no winding or burping. But if your baby does need it, gentle mini-drops (page 37) are very effective. You may also hold your baby in the safety position on your knees and gently rub his back from the base of his spine upward with your 'seat hand', while your other arm supports his chest. Mothers in many other cultures do not wind or burp their babies, but let them do so by themselves.

Constipation

Constipation causes obvious discomfort when a baby passes a stool. An increasing number of babies are affected by constipation, even when they are breastfed, which until recently was not thought to be possible. A major benefit of baby yoga is that it prevents or cures constipation.

- Practicing the hip sequence twice a day for two days usually solves the problem.

- For an older baby, twists, bends, rolling over and the upside-down sequence will help to maintain a regular elimination.

- For even quicker results if your baby has chronic constipation when you start yoga, combine the hip sequence with a warm oil massage.

Caution: if constipation is not relieved by the above suggestions, seek medical advice, and ensure that your baby is getting enough fluids.

'Yoga helped Anna a lot with her tummy ache, distracting her from her discomfort and calming her down when she was upset. Her favorite song, 'Wind the bobbin up', always made her smile. I also found rhythms of walking and breathing that she connected with just before going to sleep.'

Colic

Between about three weeks and four months of age, some otherwise healthy babies regularly experience intense abdominal pain, known as colic. An affected baby has a daily episode of excessive crying or screaming, usually in the evening, and draws up his knees in a way that indicates cramp. The term is also used to explain any distressed crying that cannot be easily pacified. Yet, one day, it comes to an end of its own accord, to everyone's relief.

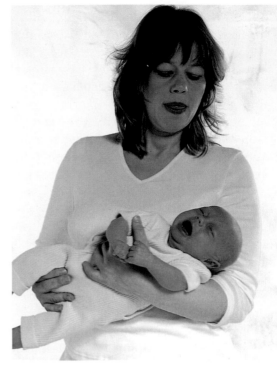

The cause of colic is unknown. It may be a spasm of the gut or a reaction of the baby's immature nervous system, or both. In yogic terms colic could be an imbalance in one of the energy centers of the body, or chakras – in this case the delicate solar plexus chakra of your baby. Colic seems to become worse if you and your baby are tired and tense. By relieving tension, yoga can soothe colic symptoms and often eliminate them.

Soothing relaxed holding

Hold your baby in the face-down safety position (page 36) against your body, but facing outward. Swivel him sideways so that his spine stretches along your rib cage, without moving your safety hand. If you are right-handed, your baby's head is to your left and your left – safety – hand comes under his left arm and your arm across his chest. If you are left-handed, your baby's head is to your right. Slide your 'seat hand' between your baby's legs so that it rests on his stomach. You can then gently massage his stomach as you walk around, in the rhythm that you would adopt for walking relaxation.

- This holding opens your baby's chest and supports his whole back against your ribs, allowing him to be spread out. This alone seems to ease the painful cramps that characterize colic.

- Although your baby is in a stretched-out position, you are holding him in a way that makes him feel very secure against your heart.

- The circular massage of his stomach is soothing, and you may hear noises indicative of digestive movement and intestinal gas.

- The rhythm of your walking is also soothing and engages you both in a joint activity. You are addressing the problem together rather than you, the parent, feeling helpless about your baby's pain.

• If you start practicing soothing holding as soon as your baby shows any signs of colic, he is unlikely to develop all the symptoms.

The hip sequence and massage

At the same time, do a full hip sequence corresponding to your baby's age, for instance in the morning, spending more time on the abdominal massage with which you make good contact with your baby at the beginning of the sequence.

To stimulate his digestion, hold your baby's feet and with your thumbs stroke the crescent lines separating the heels from the ball of each foot. This is the reflexology area for the ascending and descending colon, and will bring relief to symptoms.

Tummy stretchers

With a baby under eight weeks:

• Sit with your knees bent and place your baby on your thighs, lying on his front. Gently massage the back of his solar plexus.

• Place your baby on his front on your head.

With an older baby:

• Lie on your back with your knees up and hold your baby prone on your shins. Hold his hands and rock him gently to and fro.

• The firefighter's hold (page 91) will also effectively soothe colic.

Caution: don't place your baby across your legs, as in the roller-coaster sequence, since it seems to aggravate colic.

Soothing your solar plexus

If your baby's discomfort is making you tense, you may need to find ways to soothe your own solar plexus as well as your baby's. Once your baby is getting some relief from the soothing holding, focus on your own solar plexus chakra during joint relaxation and explore your feelings associated with this area. Life will have made its mark on it and it may be sensitive. The following affirmation, which helps you adopt a soothing attitude to yourself and your baby, has helped many parents with colicky babies: 'I can be a good listening friend to myself and my child.'

Birth and perinatal traumas

If your baby was born with life-saving interventions or needed treatment, perhaps surgery, straight after birth, it is possible that he has physical memories of pain and shock, which a triggering event can unlock unexpectedly. Even if you are not aware of any specific traumatic event but suspect it, it is best to err on the side of caution and adopt a healing approach. This cannot cause your baby any harm, and helps resolve any trauma in a practical way.

Healing a difficult birth together

If your baby's entry into the world was not as straightforward or joyful as you had hoped, you may accept the reasons with your logical mind while remaining emotionally affected on a deeper level. Interventions may have interfered with early bonding so that you find yourself having to learn to love your baby rather than falling in love with him at first sight.

Bonding through yoga

Doing yoga every day with your baby helps create a playful physical bond between you. The postures and movements engage you with him in a lively and dynamic way, and promote eye contact and communication of your reactions to each other. To create a solid bond with your baby, particularly if you were separated after the birth, try to do a routine session every day.

• Cradling is the best way to hold a baby under 12 weeks old.

• Walking relaxation and joint relaxation lying down can help you link your pregnancy to the present through a deeper closeness with your baby. They will also help you release any anger or disappointment and bring to the fore a sense of gratitude for the baby you now have, whatever your earlier experience. Talking to your baby before you enter relaxation is a way of releasing emotion that may be less threatening to him than trying to suppress it.

Treating birth injuries with yoga

Most injuries resulting from a difficult birth with intervention are minor, and heal by themselves. The following conditions respond well to yoga.

Tightness of the shoulders and arms
Your baby also refuses to open them wide and sometimes to open them at all.

- Don't force movement in any way, and don't do arm or shoulder stretches (page 58) until the situation has improved.

- Do the hip sequence followed by twists corresponding to your baby's stage of development.

- Gradually extend the twists to the shoulders. The first movement to be conceded and enjoyed is often the diagonal hand–foot stretch (page 51).

- Take a few days to consolidate each step before introducing a new one.

- Move on to action rhymes with very small movements ('Wind the bobbin up' works well), then increase the movement gradually.

- Once confidence has been gained, try the arm and shoulder sequence gently with your baby on his back.

- Wait until this has been consolidated before stretching your baby's arms in a prone position (page 59).

- Rejoice with your baby as he goes through the process of increasing his trust and opening out his chest, as he starts opening his arms more and more freely.

Misalignment of the neck
This makes the baby's head turn slightly to one side and may be painful. If you have been advised that it is not severe enough to warrant further treatment because it will right itself with time, yoga may help.

- All spinal stretches help strengthen the muscles that support the neck.

- When you do postures with your baby supine, make sure his head is straight.

- Swings in which you support your baby's head and neck are preferable to those in the face-down safety position. Continue them after 16 weeks if your arms are strong enough.

- The upside-down sequence (page 54) promotes good spinal alignment.

Healing memories of trauma

We still don't fully understand the emotional pain that fetuses and newborns might experience as a result of physical trauma. It is possible that a baby who suddenly starts screaming, without warning, may be remembering acute pain he felt earlier. (This may happen during yoga if you put slight pressure in a particular area of his body or do a specific movement no different from the day before.) The possibility is confirmed if it happens again, perhaps recurring two or three times within short intervals.

You can use yoga and more particularly the joint relaxation to soothe your baby and help him release the source of his distress from his body, whether you have identified it or not. It will have immediate results, as whatever has stirred your baby's nervous system has a chance to be resolved on a physical level. It is easier to free your baby of early trauma at this stage than later, when it is compounded by more complex memories.

Other common problems

The quality of your interaction with your baby profoundly affects his behavior, sometimes even shaping and conditioning it. If your relationship with him is sometimes negative, it is important look at this without feeling guilty or to blame, knowing that solutions are possible. The following practical suggestions will help you gain greater awareness of common negative patterns of interaction between parents and infants, and allow you to address them through yoga.

Non-stop feeding

If you take demand feeding to extremes because it seems to be the only way to pacify your baby, you may find yourself feeding him virtually non-stop, all day and sometimes at night too. The pattern is that he starts crying as soon as he has the sensation of an empty stomach, which may be about half an hour after a feed, and becomes more and more frantic until you start feeding him again. If you have taken medical advice and perhaps seen a feeding counsellor as well, and are reassured that your baby is putting on weight, you can try altering this pattern, for your own sake as well as your baby's.

- When your baby starts crying after a feed, practice the soothing relaxed holding described for colic (page 132).

- Two or three times a day when your baby is contented, do the hip sequence appropriate to your baby's development stage twice over. Talk or sing to your baby as you do it, and make it enjoyable.

- Try to relax deeply during each feed.

- Notice when your baby feeds more, and the times when he seems hungry but is easily distracted or sucks his fingers.

- Gradually space feeds more by using different yoga sequences, selecting the ones your baby enjoys most. At first, two hours between feeds will seem like a triumph. You can then aim at two-and-a-half hours, taking into account that some babies feed more frequently than others.

- Make use of your newly acquired free time to unwind, practicing energizing yoga walks (page 96) and watching your breathing.

'Failure to thrive'

When a baby 'fails to thrive', this alarming verdict may hide negative patterns of interaction existing in his environment. You may need to avoid attributing a difficult interaction with your baby to his ailments, and instead see whether any tension you feel is having an adverse effect on your baby. Although many physical ailments, for example constipation, respond well to a day or two's yoga practice, it is possible that your baby's complaint may be psychosomatic rather than merely physical. Yoga helps you perceive possible links between health and your physical or social environment, and motivates you to make constructive changes to promote harmony and well being in your life, for the benefit of both of you.

Repeating parental patterns

When you found out that you were going to become a parent, you may have felt strongly that you would do things differently from the way you were brought up, or you may have wanted to reproduce your own childhood experience for your child. Now that you are with your baby, much of this anticipation has been eclipsed by his immediate day-to-day needs. You may find yourself unwittingly replicating what you know best, which is what you experienced yourself from your parents, or deliberately doing the opposite.

Common parental patterns that new parents have difficulty with relate to structuring their baby's days and nights along 'nursery' norms; expression of emotions and communication; anxiety about doing the 'right' thing; and focus on performance over fulfillment. Developing a yoga routine with your baby helps you gain an awareness of such patterns, as you get to 'catch' yourself behaving similarly or in blatant opposition to your parent of the same sex. In relaxation particularly, as you get access to 'being', you can distance yourself from the actions of caring for your baby and understand better what shapes them. From the space of relaxation you can then feel compassion for what your parents have taught you and move on to discover more clearly your own style of parenting.

> ### Reflexology
> This therapy, which works on the principle that different parts of the feet correspond to different parts of the body, involves massage and manipulation of the feet, and helps bring about normal functioning of all the organs of the body.
>
> ### Cranial osteopathy
> This therapy involves gently manipulating the bones of the skull to treat a variety of disorders. It is often used successfully by practitioners for babies who have suffered trauma at birth, particularly after a forceps delivery.

Reversing a 'downward spiral'

Doing yoga with your baby feeds his appetite for positive experience of shared happiness between you and him. He will not be fooled by anything else than true unconditional loving. Your baby wants you to be happy, and is at his best when you are. Depression, exhaustion, unexpected challenges can, however, compromise this shared happiness and rapidly transform the expansion of joy (see page 20) into a downward spiral of doom and gloom. Reversing this downward spiral is the most valuable contribution yoga can make to your interaction with your baby.

1 Under great stress, both you and your baby experience the withdrawal of love

• Through sheer exhaustion and under extreme stress, we may at times find ourselves sinking into despair and switching off from our baby.

• Your baby then feels intensely the withdrawal of love, his source of spiritual nourishment. The more he cries, however, the worse you feel and the more he cries.

3 Accept effective support while doing yoga daily with your baby

• Whether you or your baby need special care or support through this trying time, yoga will help you create a foundation for future health based on a physical routine practiced daily.

2 Let your baby help you

• Catch a glimpse of hope in remembering that your baby still loves you unconditionally.

• Relaxing with him in this awareness may reveal to you a new world of possibilities.

4 Become aware of your interaction with your baby

• Through the principle of self-referral (page 19), you increase your awareness of the ways in which your states of mind and moods affect your baby's responses.

5 Use relaxation to neutralize and nurture your interaction with your baby.

• This is the turning point in reversing the downward spiral.

• You now start a new expanding spiral of joy, through trusting that if you really can 'let go' and surrender, your baby will respond positively. This is fragile at first, but each time your relaxation is perceived by your baby, a small change is made for the better.

6 Expansion is slow at first, but then consolidated beyond doubt.

• Whatever you go through, the foundation is such that your baby no longer experiences loss of love. Success breeds further expansion of joy and you are open to growing with your baby.

• Shared growth means renewed wonder every day, and holding your baby is a reminder that love is the stuff that binds the universe.

Index and Acknowledgments

Note: All entries relate to babies unless otherwise indicated.

Acknowledgments

My first thanks go to all the mothers, fathers and babies who volunteered to figure in this book: Ros & Ismeni Belford; Lottie Brignall; Rebecca & Monica Chapman; Sarah & Hannah Colquhoun; Katy Holt & Anthony Demetriades; Tania & Jeremy Greenfield; Angela Menzies-Walker & Alabama Nutt; Dena Lawrence & Freddie Barratt Mihranian; Sam & Molly Marshall; Clare Murphy; Marion & Aimee O'Connor; Helmut Ronniger; Pam Ha-Stevenson & Joshua; Jane & Kitty Tench; Angela & Poppy Walker, and particularly Fred, Hester & Bethsheba Tingey, who became friends through the births of their four children, and Marion who is now teaching baby yoga with Aimee.

Like all books on yoga, this book rests on a tradition passed on through many teachers. I have debt of gratitude to all: Margaret Schofield and Mary Stewart especially encouraged home practice with young children long before it was acceptable in yoga circles.

A whole production team joined forces to present baby yoga in pictures and text in the form of this book: the 'two Sarahs', Sarah Chapman, whose editing has brought much clarity and light to the text and Sarah Theodosiou, whose designing made it a visual manual, showed much equanimity in a challenging task; Pip Morgan championed the cause; Christine Hanscomb took the inspiring photographs, capturing vividly the interaction between parents and babies. Sue Duckworth is the perfect stylist.

I could not have developed baby yoga without the help and support I have received from many people over many years, too many to name but all to be thanked. Sally Lomas, who has pioneered and expanded baby yoga with Birthlight classes in Cambridge, deserves special credit. Andrea Wilson's assistance and support in the Great Ormond Street Centre have been invaluable. Pia de Filippi, Marion O'Connor and Tracey Bullock have shared the rewards and challenges of training. Suzanne Adamson's feedback and advice have enriched this book greatly. Teaching in London was made possible by the vision and support of Robin Monro, director of the Yoga Biomedical Trust, who gave babies a very warm welcome; thank you Robin.

Over the years, the trustees of Birthlight have kept me on track with unfailing generosity and confidence when books were just 'in my head'. Last, but not least, my Peruvian Amazonian sisters taught me how to handle babies, and my family has grown making space in their lives and hearts for always more babies.